WRITING YOUR FAMILY HISTORY

A practical guide

DEBORAH CASS

The Crowood Press

First published in 2004 by
The Crowood Press Ltd
Ramsbury, Marlborough
Wiltshire SN8 2HR

www.crowood.com

British Library Cataloguing-in-Publication Data
A catalogue record for this book is available from the British Library.

ISBN 1 86126 703 7

Dedication
To my grandmother, Lucy Ann Florence Ingamells Rogers (1908–78)

Acknowledgements
With grateful thanks to the following individuals for their help and support:
Andrew Peach, Mike Corr, Neil Berrett, Bob Pryor, Daphne Oldfield, the Devon Record Office, the Revd Christopher Benson, the Wiltshire Family History Society, my family and friends, and William.

Typeset by NBS Publications, Basingstoke, Hampshire, RG21 5NH

Printed and bound in Great Britain by Biddles Ltd, King's Lynn

CONTENTS

INTRODUCTION

I f you are a family historian, you almost certainly will have amassed quite a large collection of family data in the form of family trees, photographs, birth, marriage and death certificates, letters, wills and other memorabilia. In fact, the longer you conduct your research, the more you will accumulate.

Preserving a treasured collection of family papers is a headache for many genealogists and family historians – how can you both store and safely access all this material? Is your collection of family history neatly stored and indexed, perhaps using a combination of computer programs and files to store the information and documentation? Perhaps more importantly, if you do store your papers neatly and in an orderly manner, how do you give the contributors and other family members access to them, to all the fragile photographs and old letters you have collected from them over the years? Are you the family 'curator' with sole access to your material? Are you using archive-quality paper? Is your storage adequate? Is your material safe? Are there any copies? Can anyone else gain access to your computer – how will your geneology software stand the test of time?

Over the years, my concerns about my family history material grew to something bordering on neurosis. Not only was my treasured collection disintegrating with the passing of time, but what disturbed me equally was the thought of losing all this documentation through my imagined, worst-case scenarios of fire, theft or flood. Was I the only family historian who had ever tried to work out in the event of a fire how I could save both my dog and my treasured papers? They were, after all, irreplaceable, and if, like me, you have had to persuade relatives to part with their precious photographs and documents in the interests of future preservation, not only might the papers perish if personal disaster strikes, but can you really claim to keep them in any better conditions than their original owners?

If you are anything like me, far from being neatly stored and indexed, this material lives in boxes, plastic bags and old briefcases and in no particular order. In the past, as the self-appointed family historian, when I had a query from a family member or I wanted to find a piece of information, I had to wade through it all to find what I wanted. During this process, as I handled thin, fragile papers, some literally crumbling between my fingers, I was again confronted with my own mistreatment of all this material, especially when I was in a hurry to find something and when I was not as careful as I should have been.

A question perhaps even more pertinent to family historians is how will your collection papers and photographs be interpreted by future generations? Will they be able to follow your lines of research, know exactly who was who, put the right face to the right name, unravel the notes scribbled in your notebooks? Or would the many years spent researching your family history be construed by others as confusing – worse still, as meaningless – as the information lies immersed in computer programs, notebooks, albums of photographs, bags and boxes?

Until now you may have just updated family trees as babies were born and distributed the updated versions around your family as and when asked to do so. Of course, your family enjoy receiving the new record, but, apart from naming the next generation, it does nothing to impart any information or history of these ancestors. While the names will always mean something to those who remember certain characters, to future generations they will just be names.

THE SOLUTION

If you share these concerns, there is a solution, a way to bring all your research together, preserve the material you have, give all your relatives access to their family history and present your family's story in a coherent way and that is to write your family history. In writing this history not only will you be able to set the record straight as to your family's origins, but you can also detail the lives of your ancestors and use history to give them the presence they deserve. You can include facts, figures, dates, photographs and photocopies, family trees and transcriptions of original documents to share and distribute among your relatives.

This will allow access to copies of original documents to all your family members, thereby rendering unnecessary any handling of the originals and, at the same time, duplicating the material you hold, so that, should the worst happen, at least the family story would not be lost. Even more importantly, you can put your family's story into its historical context, tie up loose ends and turn names into real people by telling their stories. You will be able to offer your relatives something more than just a family tree; you will be able to share the knowledge that you have gathered and present them with the story of their family.

The 'project' of compiling the family story may give you a new focus for further research and a purpose to the gathering of your information. It may also have a positive effect on your relatives if you tell them what you are doing and yield further material for you to use.

WHY WRITE YOUR FAMILY HISTORY?

Quite apart from the advantages of saving original material, telling the story of your ancestors' lives as fully as possible, is as exciting as first discovering them from a parish register or a census return. You will also find that to document the lives of 'ordinary' people can be as worthy and extraordinary as documenting the lives of the famous. This book will show you how to give your ancestors a presence in history, whether you have comprehensive details of their lives or only limited material to work from.

It was because of the response that my own family histories received (I wrote up all three lines of my family history) and my feeling that this was the point to my research that I felt compelled to encourage other family historians to do likewise.

THE PURPOSE OF THIS BOOK

This book assumes that you have begun researching your family history – you may have been doing this for many years or for just a few months. Either way, you will most likely already have a number of guidebooks informing you of all the sources from which you can obtain your family history.

In the first chapters here you will find a list of primary sources. Although not exhaustive, these particular subjects or sources are highlighted to show their ability to provide you with material for your story. If you have not yet considered how newspaper archives and articles can help you or you have not yet delved too deeply into social or local history in your research, this is where you will be encouraged to do so. The information contained under each heading will prompt you to examine any documents that you may already hold and to explore subjects (if you have not done so already) that relate to your ancestors. I hope that these sources will ensure that you will make good use of local libraries to examine census returns, newspaper articles and local histories and your local record office for parish registers.

Then, how might your ancestors' personal possessions and gifts throw light on further material for your story? Have you ever considered questioning why a particular photograph was taken or asked for whom and what occasion a gift or family heirloom was first given or acquired? This book will illustrate how these things may become valuable sources to add interest and colour to your story.

This book, therefore, is not intended as a definitive reference guide to the major information sources – there are many other works that already do this job very well and I do not seek to replicate them (see the note at the end of the Introduction). This book is intended to take up where such guides leave you, with a wealth of accumulated information and aims to be used in conjunction with your favoured genealogical guides. You will be encouraged to write your family history using the data you have already assembled and to examine further sources. The primary aim is to show you how to use your family's history to ascertain its value in relation to telling your family story and discover a new focus and direction for your research other than merely to assemble a large database of names and dates. *Write* your family history and make a written record of your ancestors' lives to share with your relatives and future generations. In the process, it may help you to preserve your original documents and to ensure that copies of them are circulated to a wider audience. Let your documents and originals rest in their boxes and use this book to bring your family history alive.

The book will focus on:

Material

This urges you to examine what you already have and to look at further sources and their potential to provide you with information. Chapters 1 to 3 encourage you to reassess your material and cover both primary and personal sources to ensure that you examine all the traditional sources, such as birth, marriage and death certificates, National Archives and census returns; they also ensure that you cover some more unusual sources, such as the media, the Mass Observation Archive and personal possessions.

Using Limited Material to Write Your Story

Here, ways in which you can enhance your story even with limited sources are suggested. Chapter 4 is for the family historian who thinks that he or she has only very little material to go on but who still wishes to write a good account of the family history. This section may also be used by all family historians to help them to tell a more comprehensive story; there are suggestions for researching sources other than those mentioned, such as on occupations, and how to examine ancestors' relationships and comment on their health, wealth and the homes they may have lived in. This chapter also shows you how to use essays to enhance your story and it emphasizes the use of local and social history.

How to Write and Present Your Story

Chapters 5 and 6 set out recommendations on how you might actually put the words on the page and offer suggestions on how you could start your story and where it might end and on speculating on our earliest ancestors. There is also advice on style, format and binding and on how you might wish to publish the finished product.

In places, I have used some of my own family research to illustrate just how valuable the information you may acquire from a particular source could be to your story.

A Final Note on Sources

While the sources referred to in this book are mainly British, the principle of obtaining as much information as possible from any similar source in another country is the same. Wherever you may live and of whatever culture you may be, you can apply the advice and suggestions contained here to your own family history.

For further guidance on sources (books, periodicals, addresses, telephone numbers and websites), see the appendices starting on page 112.

1 AN OVERVIEW OF PRIMARY SOURCES

In order to write a family history you first need to have material. You have to know as much about your subject – your family – as possible. Material in the form of names and dates forms the 'bones', the skeleton of your family history. Letters, photographs, memories and anecdotes are what you will need to add 'flesh'. Even if you have only a limited source of these, the use of local and social history will add interest and enrich your story in the absence of other family material to draw upon.

Neither do you need to have a long family history in order to justify writing it. If your family history is in its early stages, you can still start to write a comprehensive history of the lives and times of your relatives – a good story does not necessarily need a host of ancestors. You may wish to start writing your history with yourself and work backwards. If this has the effect of putting you off, then you may wish to start with your parents or grandparents. If you have a fairly extensive family history you might like to start writing it from the farthest point and work towards the present.

Whether writing an extensive history involving many ancestors or just one of your immediate family, material is the key to making it interesting to your reader. In your quest for family material do not overlook those relatives nearest to you in generation just because they may not be particularly old; they will almost certainly have a wealth of material, anecdotes and stories which it would be a pity to ignore. Likewise, do not be afraid to approach an old aunt or uncle you have lost touch with who could possibly provide you with much information of relevance.

Your family history material will come from many sources and it may surprise you just how many you have from which to seek the information you need:

- birth, death and marriage certificates
- parish registers
- parish records
- census returns
- National Archives/local record offices
- wills
- local history

- social history
- reference books
- newspaper articles/news items
- family memories/anecdotes
- local libraries
- photographs
- personal correspondence
- possessions/gifts
- diaries
- hobbies
- relatives
- Mass Observation archive
- surname studies
- the Internet

All of these and their ability to provide you with material for your family story are covered here, and although this tally is not exhaustive, it could be used as a checklist for research into your family's past. The categories are divided into two main areas: some I have referred to as *primary sources* since these are the obvious ones you would look at; the secondary sources I have referred to as *personal sources* as these are the ones that will be closest to your personal family history, such as diaries and correspondence, all or some of which your relatives or ancestors may have had and that may provide the more intimate insights and interesting minutiae of their lives. Writing your family history is a chance to revisit all the data you have and to analyse it and pull out the information to form your story.

BIRTH, MARRIAGE AND DEATH CERTIFICATES

Since 1 July 1837 records of all births, marriages and deaths have been subject to national official registration by civil authorities; they record the events and issue the appropriate certificates. The civil registration system provides family historians with an indispensable resource for tracing their ancestors back to that date and will most likely form the backbone of the skeleton upon which you can begin to build up your family's story. Indexes to these records may be found at the Family Record Centre in London, some record offices, local history libraries and through the Internet.

Birth Certificates
These provide a mine of information and a starting point for the family history writer. A birth certificate, for example, will give you the name of your relative, usually his or her parents, and where and when your relative was born. After some simple research into the facts contained on a birth certificate you will be able to add to the circumstances surrounding your relative's birth.

Date of Birth

The date on which your relative was born will enable you to place him or her in history. You will be able to check for any significant events that may have occurred on or around that date and be able to inform your readers which monarch was reigning at the time, the Prime Minister then in office, what were the burning issues of the day and the more pertinent local details that could have affected your relative's life.

Name

The name of your relative could help you in unexpected ways by confirming family ties. For example, my illegitimate great-grandfather Isaac Brown Rogers was named after his father Isaac Brown, even though the father's name did not appear on the birth certificate. The Christian name may also reflect the importance of the mother's family, with the mother's maiden name being used as a Christian name for a child or the mother's father's name being used in its entirety for continuity. As an example, an ancestor of mine called her son Richard Dawson Carey Ingamells after her father, Richard Dawson Carey. Where this occurs, it could be an indication of the recent death of a relative and the naming of the next son or daughter being made by way of remembrance of the individual. This may link you unexpectedly with the next generation of your family. Perhaps you have instances where a first-born male or female always carry a certain name; it is highly likely that the further your research takes you that reused Christian names will appear in your family history. Names of ancestors are worth a second look to determine the existence of any patterns or links to previous generations.

Place of Birth

The place of birth is an interesting fact to bring to notice – placing your relatives in a particular place and perhaps even social standing. The location of a birth will enable you to trace a map of the area, locate a street or road and maybe even find a photograph of it from local archives. If your relative was born at home, you may wish to describe and comment on what sort of housing it was, when it was constructed, whether it is still there and, if it is, provide a photograph, all matters of interest in your story. (*See* Hearth and Home in Chapter 4.)

Parents' Names

The certificate will show the names of the father and mother, or only the mother's name if your relative was born illegitimately. If the father's name is omitted, this will restrict your research on this line of your story, leaving you to concentrate on the maternal line. If the parents were married, the mother's maiden name will also appear, giving you an opportunity to enlarge your story by introducing the mother's family.

Marriage Certificates

Marriage certificates can introduce you to many people linked to your relatives. As well as the bride and groom, there are their fathers and the witnesses. The certificate will also show occupations and addresses.

Ages

The ages of your newly weds may feature on the certificate or may be written as 'over 21' or 'full age'. Do not always taken the ages at face value but check them against their birth certificates or census returns. This may be worth commenting on in your story, especially if there is a disparity. For example, in the 1851 census my relatives are shown as aged 21 and 16, and yet two months later their marriage certificate shows both of full age. Since they did not marry in their nearest church, it begs me to ask the question: did they have parental consent or did they elope? Where possible, always check the ages since, who knows, you may be able to comment on a romantic elopement. Bear in mind that parents' or guardians' permission to marry was still needed for anyone aged under 21 until 1969, when the age was lowered to 18.

Occupations

Occupations will provide you with a rich source of information. If your ancestors were town- or city-based then they were likely to have industrial occupations, maybe factory workers, coal miners or dock workers, information on all of which can be obtained from reference and history books or through research in your local library. Some sources may also give you the wages paid in the past, the conditions people worked in and the working methods used, all of which are important when researching the lives of your relatives and explaining their working environments (*See* the section on Occupations in Chapter 4.)

Residence

Note the residence of your ancestor and check it against any others that you may have found them at already. Also note the residence of the intended spouse and the proximity of the two addresses: did they live in the same town or village, around the corner from one another, or come from places further afield?

Witnesses

Do not overlook the witnesses on the marriage certificate. Although the names may be unknown to you, they could have been your relatives' best friends. If the names are familiar, research should tell you whether a witness was the bride's or the groom's brother or sister, or some other family member; either way, the names could be important and confirm the family unit, especially in extended families where members of which do not all share the same surname.

For example, people today may think that the extended family unit is a modern development, the product of divorce and of people having several marriages, when, in fact, extended families were nothing unusual to older generations. While it is probably more the case that extended families came about due more to widowhood than divorce, my own experience seems even more strange; in 1860 my great-great grandmother was apparently 'left' by her parents to be brought up by strangers in Mountain Ash, Wales, when they moved from their village of Evercreech in Somerset. This relative lived in her new household from the age of 6 with neither of her real parents' being evident on census returns. She appears to have been brought up in the household of a Mr and Mrs Rogers, who had no apparent family ties. In the 1861 census return, aged 6, she was described as a visitor, but ten years later she was still there.

By the time she was married, Mr Rogers was a widower and my great-great grandmother was referring to him as her 'father'. It seems that she also returned Rogers's generosity because he continued to live with her and her husband William Mogg, in a household that also consisted of her illegitimate son (my great-grandfather, to whom she gave the surname Rogers), her father-in-law and the three daughters from her marriage. Luckily for me, one of these daughters, Harriett Mogg, appeared as a witness on my great-grandfather's marriage certificate, confirming that, although he did not share her surname, my illegitimate great-grandfather indeed belonged to that rather complicated family unit.

Men and women took on other people's children and families as their own, if not through divorce then by the death of one partner and the remarriage of the survivor, and therefore witnesses at marriages may not always be as obscure as they appear. Indeed, to keep track of extended families of step-sisters and step-brothers, and mothers and fathers in multiple marriages can be like unravelling genealogical wool. As the example above illustrates, relationships could be as complex in the past as they can be perceived to be today and so it is worth taking the time to study the names of marriage witnesses.

Death Certificates
Death certificates reveal to you the end of your relative's life. They will tell you where and when and from what cause your relative died, and who, if anyone, was in attendance at the end (sometimes another way of confirming family units – daughters- or brothers-in-law could be present at the time).

Place of Death
The majority of people in the nineteenth century were born and died at home and the locations of these will tell you much about your relatives' lives. Some people never left the town or village they were born in and just moved around in it, living in various houses or tenements. Your relative may have died in an almshouse or workhouse; if this was the case, again, you will be provided with an opportunity for further research and material on which to comment and include in your story. The buildings of such institutions as workhouses or

almshouses may still be standing, allowing you to add a photograph of the place where your ancestor died.

Cause of Death
You will also learn the cause of your relation's death and this too can lead to a mine of information. If he or she was unfortunate enough to die from one of the prevailing diseases of the time, such as cholera, typhoid or diphtheria, a little local history research should reveal whether there was a particular epidemic at the time. Depending on how thorough you want to be, you could discover an explanation of the disease and even its progression when once caught. This may seem a little morbid, but the occurrence of such diseases is luckily mostly a thing of the past now and their appearance in your account could raise a question from those who do not know along the lines of, 'What was diphtheria?'

Your relative may have suffered a violent or otherwise unexpected death which may have been the subject of an inquest. If this was the case, this event will have almost certainly been reported in a local newspaper at the time and it would be worth trawling through it on either side of the date of your relative's death. The death certificate of my great-great grandfather revealed that he drowned in the Solent. The cause of death was stated as 'Accidentally drowned during a storm whilst on a coal barge.' The certificate also gave the date of the subsequent inquest.

Obtaining Details of Inquests
Depending on the time lapse since your relative died, if an inquest was required, you may even be able to obtain a copy of the inquest papers (a 75-year rule applies). These may be stored at your local record office, but if not, you may find the Gibson Genealogical Guide Coroners Records helpful in locating them.

From the present day back to 1837, civil registration will be your guiding light to a succession of ancestors.

PARISH REGISTERS AND BISHOPS' TRANSCRIPTS

Pre-1837 Civil Records
Before 1837, the registration of baptisms, marriages and burials in England and Wales was conducted by using the parish register system. This system began in 1538, but the records dating back to that time may be patchy. Luckily for the family historian today, in 1598 the Elizabethans decreed that the parish priest should make a copy of the entries in the parish register for submission to his bishop, thus creating the Bishops' Transcripts. These may prove useful in cases where the original parish register has been lost or destroyed. You can locate parish registers at your County Record Office and Bishops' Transcripts at either the former or the Diocesan Record Office. Check with your County Record Office before you go there to ensure that they hold the registers for the

[Printed by authority of the Registrar General.]

HC 163280

D. Cert.
S.R.

CERTIFIED COPY of an ENTRY OF DEATH
Pursuant to the Births and Deaths Registration Act 1953

Registration District   PORTSMOUTH

1908 . Death in the Sub-district of   PORTSMOUTH & MID SOUTHSEA   in the   COUNTY OF PORTSMOUTH C.B.

No.	When and where died	Name and surname	Sex	Age	Occupation	Cause of death	Signature, description, and residence of informant	When registered	Signature of registrar
1	2	3	4	5	6	7	8	9
355	1st September 1908 — In Cowes Roads The Solent	James CASS	Male	60 years	Bargeman of 33 Derby Road Stanshaw	Accidentally drowned during a storm whilst on a coal barge	Certificate received from T.A.Bramsdon Coroner for Portsmouth Inquest held September 14th 1908	Sixteenth September 1908	S.M.Clark

Certified to be a true copy of an entry in a register in my custody.

[signature]   Superintendent Registrar.

12th June 1989   Date

CAUTION:—It is an offence to falsify a certificate or to make or knowingly use a false certificate or a copy of a false certificate intending it to be accepted as genuine to the prejudice of any person, or to possess a certificate knowing it to be false without lawful authority.

The death certificate of James Cass, who drowned during a storm.

parish you are interested in and to book your seat. Welsh registers are in the National Library of Wales or the Welsh county record offices.

If your family history research has already taken you past civil registration then you will be familiar with parish registers. However, civil registration after 1837 provided certain checks and balances to ensure that you had the right ancestor, parish records do not . But there is a lifeline here if you find multiple possibilities in parish registers for your next ancestor and that is in checking to see whether he or she appears on the International Genealogical Index and using this tool to help in the process of elimination (*see* the International Genealogical Index on p.23).

If your experience involving parish registers is anything like mine, you may have to travel some distance to your preferred County Record Office, and possibly to another county altogether. Each volume I opened would give me a mixed feeling of excitement and fear – akin, I would imagine, to opening a treasure chest – the anticipation of what you might find inside but also the fear that it could be empty. Time disappears ever so quickly in a record office when searching through parish registers and, spending hours in deciphering sometimes illegible old handwriting, with eyes out on stalks so that you do not miss a thing. The rewards of finding an elusive baptism or burial entry, however, more than make up for the effort required.

Scottish and Irish Records

Scottish parish registers generally begin in the 1690s and may be found in the General Record Office for Scotland for contact details). Many southern Irish records were destroyed by fire in 1922 and therefore the National Archives and the National Library of Ireland should be consulted for the availability of these. The Public Record Office in Belfast should be consulted for records relating to Northern Ireland.

Points to Remember
The records relate to baptisms as opposed to births, and to burials as opposed to deaths, so these will not be the dates of birth or death. Apart from this, you can use the registers as in much the same way as the civil registration certificates, to glean as much information as possible – accepting, of course, that the information available is not so plentiful as in civil registration. Ensure that you record every detail, and that includes the year and the parish in which you have made your discovery. This is especially important if you are copying all instances of your surname and may save you a return journey. Even scant details could provide you with clues to your ancestors' past (*see* Chapter 4).

OTHER PARISH RECORDS

Parish records will be located at the County Record Office within the county you are researching. The list below gives some idea of the records that may be found there:

- poor relief expenditure books
- churchwardens' accounts and rates
- settlement papers
- apprenticeship indentures
- bastardy papers/records

Parish records can shed light on your ancestors' lives and time spent at your local county archive may be usefully spent. As an illustration of what you might turn up, below is a copy of an apprenticeship indenture of Elizabeth Carnell, a great-great-great-grandmother of my husband, who was apprenticed to a farmer, Gilbert Pinsent in Kingsteignton, Devon in 1812. Elizabeth was 11 years old at the time and, in a manner that conjures up Dickens's *Oliver Twist*, was 'apprenticed' to the farmer until she was 21 years old or married (with Pinsent's permission). She would have been expected to learn about housekeeping and husbandry in return for her clothing, board and lodgings. Most apprentices were used as little more as cheap labour, but, according to family history, Elizabeth must have used her time at the farm well because she became very knowledgeable about herbs and made her own creams and potions. Unfortunately, the farmer's learning did not extend to teaching her how to read and write and therefore nothing of her acquired wisdom was ever written down.

Census Returns

As a family historian, you will already be aware that census returns can provide excellent genealogical information for every ten years from 1841. Census returns will provide you with:

- a street name and number (although the numbers do not always correspond to those in the same road today)
- a list of all the inhabitants in the house
- their names
- their ages
- their occupations
- their places of birth (this is especially useful for anyone not born in the county in which he or she lived).

Ensure that you re-examine the information you already have from census returns in order to extract the maximum value from this source.

From this source you could provide yourself with the birth certificates of all named children, which would give you a place of birth for each, by which means you could track how your relatives may have moved during the period covered by these data.

It will also say whether children were 'scholars' or at work; for example, an 11-year-old might be described as a miner but a 10-year-old as still a scholar –

1812 apprenticeship indenture of Elizabeth Carnell, aged 11.

a fact that would be interesting in a family history when compared with today's society. You may even be able to comment on the schooling a relative received, whether from a poor school or a private one and local archives could yield further facts.

Census returns may also give details of other people or relatives living in the same household as your relatives; for example, a grandfather or grandmother might also have lived in the house, or a brother, sister or a child from a previous marriage. If you have knowledge about the type of housing they lived in, counting the people living in one house will give an insight into their domestic lives. I know that my great-great-great grandparents bought up a family of nine in a two-up, two-down cottage in Shaftesbury and another set of great-great grandparents had their in-laws living with them all their married lives. And do not forget to look and see who lived next door – this could add to the picture.

NATIONAL ARCHIVES

The National Archives (now incorporating the Public Record Office [PRO] and the Historical Manuscripts Commission) comprise the United Kingdom's national collection. They hold thousands of records that are of potential interest to family historians, including:

- military records
- some police service documents
- records of merchant seamen
- emigration and immigration details
- maps and photographs.

The National Archives have also produced a range of booklets entitled *Pocket Guides to Family History*, which can be found in the Appendix. Addresses for all the British National Archives repositories may also be found there.

If you have access to the internet you can gain access to the National Archives at Kew, which will provide a guide to everything available. This site is particularly helpful if you are planning a visit to the National Archives and time is limited. You can use the site to refine your search before you go, allowing you to arm yourself with the reference numbers of the documents you wish to examine. There are also two further linkeed sites which can help you in tracing documents.

The records of the National Archives helped me to trace the career of my great-grandfather when all I had was a photograph of him in naval uniform. The photograph was in a very bad condition and had been given to me by a relative after I had conducted many years of family research. I could hardly believe that, after all this time, I should possess such a photograph, as I had long given up hoping a photograph of him might exist. Although grateful, I was a bit sceptical and mindful that, although it was given to me in good faith

Harry Cass's naval record.

as being my great-grandfather, there was always a chance that I could be looking at someone completely unrelated to my family; after all, no one in the family had ever mentioned the existence of this photograph before. I studied it and around the sailor's hat he wore, the name of a ship was just discernible – HMS *King George V*.

A chance comment to a friend who frequented the Archive about this yielded dividends. On her next visit my friend looked up the crew lists for *King George V* and found my great-grandfather's name, along with a description of him and his date and place of birth, all of which I was able to confirm. Since he both joined and left this ship in 1917, it was also possible to work out that he was 32 years old at the time the photograph was taken. My friend was also able to obtain a photocopy of this information for me. Thus a rapidly deteriorating photograph of my relative provided just enough information to shed light on his First World War career in the Navy, all of which was waiting to be discovered in the National Archives.

If you have ancestors who have been in the military services, a visit to the National Archive or its website is essential in gaining more material for your history. As well as being a national repository, a number of documents are made available for viewing on line. Check their website for an up-to-date list of papers available in this format.

INTERNATIONAL GENEALOGICAL INDEX (IGI)

If your research has come to a dead end by taking you back beyond the start of civil registration in 1837, then you can try the IGI, organized by the Church of the Latter Day Saints – otherwise known as the Mormon Index – to set you on your way again. The IGI for England and Wales has been compiled by using a range of information, including parish registers, and is listed in alphabetical order county by county. This having been said, by no means all parishes are covered, but if your ancestors tended not to stay in one place for very long – and many of them did not – then it would be a good place at which to start.

The IGI can be accessed by microfiche or CD-ROM in large libraries, in the Church of the Latter-day Saints Family History Centre and the Family Records Centre (details in the Appendix). With the IGI you may be able to trace ancestors throughout a county, the country or the world (*see* Surname Studies later in this chapter.) You can obtain a print-out of the surnames you are interested in and gain a good idea of the spread of your particular surname across a county and across the country as a whole. It could certainly prove useful in tracking down elusive ancestors and helping to establish family groups by baptisms.

WILLS

Wills are a fascinating source of information for the family historian. They may provide you with the means to study your relative's possessions and relationships (especially within extended families) and even get an idea of the money they kept under their mattresses.

Copies of wills of ancestors who lived in the sixteenth and the seventeenth century were given to me by a fellow researcher early in my quest for family history and I was amazed at the detail they contained about my relatives' lives. While I had no physical images of them, by virtue of the facts they wrote down at the end of their lives I gained an insight into their world. Without the wills such details would have been lost forever.

As well as revealing their wealth and possessions, they also show how God-fearing and religious people were. The next two examples from my own family show that first and foremost, before any earthly legacies were bestowed, they recorded their entreaties for God's forgiveness and offered him their bodies and souls. From one of my ancestors, Christopher Ingamells, came this humble plea:

> In the name of God in the fourteenth day of April one thousand six hundred and ninety two, I Christopher Ingamells of South Reston in the County of Lincoln husbandman being sick in body but of good and perfect

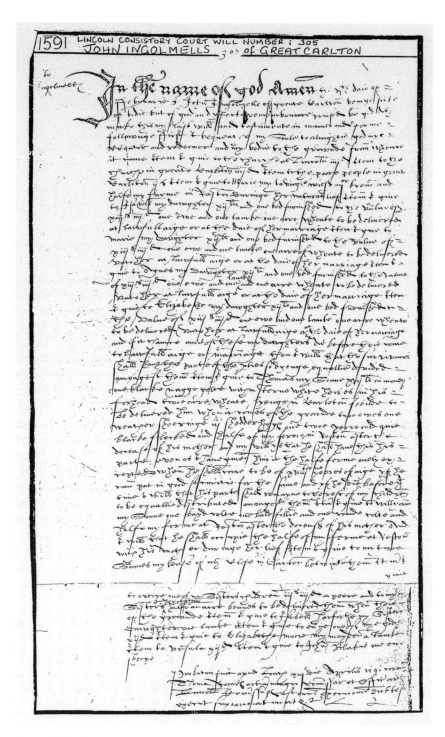

The Will of John Ingolmells, 1591.

memory, thanks be to almighty God. This my last will in testament ... And first being sorry from the bottom of my heart for my sins past most humbly ask forgiveness for the same I give and commit my soul unto Almighty God my saviour redeemer in whom and by the merits of Jesus Christ I trust and believe to be saved and by body to the earth from whence I come taken to be therein decently interred according to the discretion of my executor herein after named ...

In the will of Thomas Yngamells of Saleby in 1538 he makes provision for the 'praying of his soul' in church as follows:

In the name of God amen the 1st day of March the year of our Lord God 1538, I Thomas Yngamells of the parish of Saleby hale of mind and good rememberance makes thee my last testament and will in the manner and form following. First I bequeath my soul to Almighty God, Our Lady Saint Mary and all the saints. Item I bequeath to the blessed sacrament in the foresaid church 4 pence. Item to bequeath to our Lady in our mother church 4 pence. Item I bequeath to the church nave of Saleby 21 pence. Item I bequeath to the reparations of St Peter's Church 4 pence. Item I bequeath to the guild of St Margaret's in the parish of Saleby one acre of wheat ...

Unless you were a widow, single woman or heiress, the ability to make a will was confined to men as the heads of households. As a widow living in the time of the Cromwell's government, Elizabeth Ingomels (*see* box on p.26) appears more than capable of arranging her affairs; indeed, she must have possessed the mind of an accountant to work out to whom and how much and at what stages she had bequeathed her money.

This will had been transcribed from a photocopy of the original; it was fascinating to look at and stirred my imagination. How she had possibly worked all her figures out was food for thought – this was no deathbed declaration, she was unlikely to have worked out whom to give what to when she was about to die. There was no mention of her being sick, so I suggested that she was extremely well organized in her affairs. I could imagine her, seated at a heavy oak table with a lighted taper, ink pot and quill, while someone sat close by putting down all the names of her beneficiaries and the amounts that she wished to leave them (she could not write, her will was simply signed by her mark). This was the picture I drew for my readers and could not have been too far from the truth.

When studying wills consider the era that they were made in; for example, in the case of another ancestor, he had made his will in 1547 but died two years after. After studying the political climate at the time he wrote the will, I discovered that Henry VIII had just died and I drew attention to this fact and that a period of social unrest was expected with the accession of a child king (Edward IV was nine when he succeeded Henry VIII); this could have been why my ancestor considered it was prudent to make a will at that time.

If you have wills to use as a source, note their dates and see whether anything was happening locally or nationally that might have affected your ancestors to draw them up. Note whether they claimed that they were 'sick of body' (an indication that they may have been told that they were dying), and, where possible, try to find any burial references from parish records.

The Will of Elizabeth Ingomels

March 13th 1650

In the name of God Amen I Elizibeth Ingomels of Great Carlton in ye county of Lincoln widow do make and ordain this my last will and testament in manner and form following. First I give and bequeath my soul to almighty God my maker and to Jesus Christ my sancifier and preserver and my body to the earth from whence it was taken praying to be saved amongst the rest and my body to be buried in the Churchyard of the Town aforesaid. Item I give to the poor of the parish five shillings to be paid within a month after my decease. Item I give in charity four shillings within a year after my decease. Item I give to my daughter Elizabeth Webster and her five daughters every one of them four shillings and her son James two shillings all to be paid within a year after my decease. Item I give to my daughter Esibell four shillings and her two children five shillings to be paid within a year of my decease. Item I give to my son Thomas Ingomels four shillings and his daughter two shillings and his son twelve pence all to be paid within a year next after my decease. Item I give to my son Henry Clark's two sons and within either of them, my ewes and lambs and twenty shillings a year to be paid within a year and a half next after my decease. Item I give to my daughter Francis Clark a blanket, a coverlet, a sheet, a pillow and half the brass and pewter table and five shillings to be paid within the month after my decease. Item I give to my daughter's son Robert Clark ten shillings to be paid within a year and a half after my decease and I give to Thomas William Clark son's to Henry Clark a calf of a year old at Mayday. Item I give to John Ingomels and Francis and Faith every one of them five shillings to be paid out of my land within three months after my decease. Item my son Henry Clark my little half acre of beans. Item I do appoint my executor to pay to John Ingomels four pounds that his father did for the building of my barne and to pay to Brian Brown's children ten shillings that his father did pay and my will is that my son Christopher shall have all my houses and land to me belonging provided that my son Henry Clark and his wife shall have three dwellings in the house for one whole year after my decease paying no rent for that Year. Item I bequeath to George Furth's wife two shillings to be paid within that month next after my decease. All the rest of goods unbequeathed my funeral being discharged I give to my son Christopher whom I make my sole supervisor of this last will and testament where unto I have given my hand. The day and year above written Widow Ingomels.

Comparing Monetary Values

Comparing such values from the past with today's figures is difficult due to inflation, but you could find some prices of goods at the time to make comparison easier and more useful. For example taking the will of Elizabeth Ingomels, when she was bequeathing her money £5 bought a sword with a silver hilt, 27s bought a round mahogany table, £6 was the annual wage of a housemaid and 1/2d bought you half a loaf.

Repositories for Wills

In the case of early wills, the National Archives at Kew should be your first port of call. For wills made since 1858 contact the Principle Registry of the Family Division.

GRAVESTONES AND INSCRIPTIONS

If you know where a relative was buried and there is still a gravestone there, make reference to it in your history and a note of the inscription and its location.

Some inscriptions provide a little more detail than might be expected; for example, relatives of mine died during the Second World War, and an inscription that long fascinated me as a child told how they were killed by the last V1 rocket to fall on Portsmouth. It is also not unusual for earlier gravestones to include the name of the street your ancestor lived in and the cause of death – for example, typhoid or influenza – this is especially so when a whole family may have perished over a short period.

If you find an entry for your ancestor in a parish register and he or she was from a poor community, the chances are that there will be no gravestone for you to discover. In all cases, always check with the local family history society since a great deal of work has been done around the country in preserving the inscriptions on tombs and gravestones before they become too weathered, are destroyed altogether, or are simply removed. It may also be the case that, having discovered the record of an ancestor's burial in the parish records, the graveyard itself may have disappeared and been redeveloped. I know of a cemetery in Portsmouth which once contained many old gravestones but is now part of the ferry terminal.

WAR GRAVES AND MEMORIALS

The locations of war graves may be found through the Commonwealth War Graves Commission. The Commission's website is very well constructed and professional and may provide you with more information than you might have expected. Access to it, giving the location of the grave of your relative, is free and includes provision for a broad search to be made if you do not know the specific details, such as of the date of death or the regiment or unit of your relative. It is possible therefore for you to make a name search,

In Memory of
Guardsman HENRY EDWARD DAVIS

2623517, 1st Bn., Grenadier Guards
who died age 20
on 11 August 1944
Son of Thomas and Florence Mary Davis, of
Stamshaw, Portsmouth, Hants.

Remembered with honour
ST. CHARLES DE PERCY WAR CEMETERY

Commemorated in perpetuity by
the Commonwealth War Graves Commission

Certificate available from the Commonwealth War Graves Commission website.

although, if you do this, be prepared for results showing multiple occurrences of the same name. The results sometimes give the names of the parents, which obviously help to confirm that you have the right person. If you find your relative among the records you can print or copy a certificate such as the one shown.

The website will also provide details of the cemetery, the grave or the reference number of the memorial and visiting and historical information, which may include a précis of the action in which your relative fell; this is extremely helpful if you were otherwise unaware. At a small cost, you could purchase from the Commission a schedule of the cemetery which will detail exactly where your ancestor is buried and is especially useful if you plan to visit.

SURNAME STUDIES

Origins of Your Family Name

You could use your research into the origins of your family name as the basis of beginning your family history (*see* Chapter 5). There are many books on the origins of surnames, so if your family name features in any of these you could use this source to add interest to your story.

It was the need to distinguish one person from another because of the limited range of surnames used by the Normans that led to the adoption of additional names. Surnames were derived from:

- occupations (Wheeler, Cartwright, Taylor, Carpenter, Archer)
- nicknames (Greengrass – green as grass, Little or Large – in stature)
- place names (Hampton, Skipton, Field)
- son of ... (Jameson, Johnson, Robinson).

Geographic Distribution

It could be that your surname is linked to a particular county or area. This may be the case with the more unusual surnames since they may derive from a particular place name or simply be unique to an area. I was particularly lucky in this respect when following my Ingamells ancestors, who have already appeared in this chapter. The name seemed to emanate from Ingoldmells on the east coast in Lincolnshire, and, indeed, every instance of the name led back there, making it a name unique to the county. Even those sharing the name in the USA and Australia will eventually trace their ancestry back to Lincolnshire. The IGI, described above, could help you to pursue this line of enquiry.

One-Name Studies

There are now many groups that have formed from one-name studies, where people who all share the same surname or derivatives of it from across the world share information and sometimes have gatherings. You may wish to consider contacting one of these if you find one with your surname or set one up, contact The Guild of One-Name Studies (GOONS).

Changes and Variations in Surnames

It is worth remembering a quotation from Debrett's *Guide to Tracing Your Ancestry*: 'There is a reluctance to accept variations in the spelling of a surname, forgetting that at a time when reading and writing were at best a rare effort for many people ... and even Shakespeare spelt his name in four different ways.'

When using the IGI you will see that variations on a surname are also listed, so you may wish to comment on this. In my own family I have examples of a change and of variations in a surname. During the nineteenth century, what was 'Case' in Shaftesbury, Dorset, became 'Cass' in Portsmouth. I concluded, after establishing that I was looking at the correct family, that possibly the local dialect had something to do with the recording of it and that, when my relative moved, it became Cass. This is a point worth considering, especially if your ancestors moved from one area of the country to another – try saying their surname with a different accent to see how it would sound in another region.

In another example, one of my great-great grandmothers simply assumed a family name! When I knew my great-grandfather's name was Isaac Brown Rogers and that he was illegitimate, I naturally assumed his mother's surname would be Rogers. But Rogers was a name she had 'borrowed' from the people she was apparently left in the care of. The father of her illegitimate son was Isaac Brown and so she left no one in any doubt of this when she called him Isaac Brown. But she obviously was in a quandary since her surname was Green, and so I suppose that her reluctance to call her son Isaac Brown Green was understandable, hence she borrowed the name Rogers. Therefore it is a family name but with no real family history to it. It just goes to show you that you can take nothing for granted when researching family history.

Losing the Family Name and Branching Off

In the light of my own experience, it seems likely that the family name you have now may not have been the name of an ancestor, say in 1066; certainly you have an ancestor going back to that time, but under what name? You may find that your research ends quite abruptly with one name, and that to reach further back you need to follow a new branch, with a new name. You should not be put off by this – the family tree of the Royal Family shows how differing names enter to take the lineage back into time. If you lose trace of the family name, pick up another branch to see whether you can make better progress.

2 Further Sources

Your local library will in all probability house all manner of material about the locality in which you live or your ancestors once did, bearing in mind that the size of the library will reflect the volume and the variety of the material held. If your library is small you may not be provided with much information and you may have to travel to a larger library to find more comprehensive local archives. Typically, if you have access to a large library you are likely to find the following research aids:

- local history
- social history
- reference books
- street maps
- street and trade directories
- internet access
- newspaper archives.

I was lucky enough to have the excellent and enormous Portsmouth library when beginning my research and was introduced early to the value of census records and newspaper and local archives as sources. There was also a wealth of history on the development of the city from when records began, including early street maps and directories listing the inhabitants, which was particularly useful in tracking the movements of my relatives since they seemed to move almost on a yearly basis to different rented accommodation.

Your library may also hold runs of family history magazines and be able to point you towards local history groups. These may be particularly useful if you do not live near where your ancestors came from, and such groups may be able to guide you towards unsuspected information sources.

It is also important to remember the inter-library lending service through which books from other county libraries may be lent, although there will be a small charge for this.

LOCAL HISTORY

You cannot write a family history without becoming involved in local history, it is central to uncovering your relatives' lives – where they lived and what they did. From studying it you will glean information about where your relatives lived – their street, road or lane, when the houses were built, the local economy – agricultural or industrial, the very factors that would have affected their everyday lives (*see* Hearth and Home in Chapter 4).

So many of today's towns and cities have been rebuilt that street maps, especially if the street plan in which you are interested is no longer there, will shed light on where your relatives lived. Local history books with old photographs will help if a relative's house is no longer standing. My great-grandfather's house in Shaftesbury had been rebuilt in the 1950s among a row of old cottages. We thought that perhaps the one he had lived in had just crumbled into the ground, but we discovered that this was not the case. We found a book on the local history with plenty of photographs and there was a picture, taken in 1950, of the fire that had destroyed his and two other cottages when a local decorator had used a blowtorch and set the thatch and the cottages on fire. The cottages had been replaced by modern housing, but it explained what had happened and also showed us a picture of the cottage where he had lived in the aftermath of the fire.

When you discover that your relatives hailed from a particular locality it is a good idea to visit it and try to find the street where they lived. Not only will you discover for yourself their village or town, but you will be returning to where your ancestors came from and be able to walk down their street, stand outside their house and know for certain that they were there. While you are there also call at the local newsagents and libraries and search for local history books or a local photographic history, and, while you are in the library, ask whether there are any local history groups (*see* Visiting Ancestral Places in Chapter 3). Once you have located where your ancestors lived you will be able to look more closely at their community; this is where you will find the benefit of local history research.

SOCIAL HISTORY

Social history will be your treasure chest of information about your ancestors' daily lives. You cannot write a family history without becoming involved in social history – the key to how we used to live (*see* Using Essays in Chapter 4). It will enable you to place your relative in a particular time in history. Even the most basic study will provide you with information such as name of the monarch on the throne at the time your ancestor lived and the politics and socio-economic climate then prevailing which might have affected his or her life (*see* the sections on Migration and Emigration in Chapter 4). The study of social history will allow you to comment on your relative's life in more depth, especially in relation to an individual's occupation and working conditions. A little research will provide you with a detailed knowledge of the conditions in, for example, textile factories, farming and mining, and of how a workhouse operated.

Luckily for family history writers, there is a wealth of material that can be used to illustrate the lives and times of their ancestors. There is also a growing thirst for knowledge of how our predecessors lived, which not only means that more of such information is available, but also that it is much more readily absorbable and interesting. This is in no small part due to the more frequent televising of history programmes, including even dedicated channels, which has brought new life to the subject. Presenters such as Simon Schama and David Starkey have injected an enthusiasm into history that has broadened its appeal. Those with access to the Internet will also, given sufficient patience, find much of value to them.

Social history is an essential component of your family history and, when commenting on one aspect of your family's life, it is difficult not to be drawn into another.

As an example of how you can use social history material, both my grandfather and great-grandfather had worked down the coal mines in South Wales. My great-grandfather became a miner aged 11 in 1888 and my grandfather (William Cromwell Rogers) at 13 in 1914. I wanted to give my readers an understanding of what their life would have been like in the mines between 1888 and 1926. I had a second-hand account from an uncle who had questioned his father as to his mining experiences (*see* Chapter 3):

He used to tell me they used to mine a couple of ton of coal. If they mined two tons they would only pay them for one ton because they would say that so much was shell, so much was rock, and it must have been frustrating when you know you've worked hard to mine two or three ton and then for them to take half of it off you, and you had no redress, you couldn't go to anybody, so this is how they formed the Unions ...The coal mines used to own all the shops and the houses, so when they mined the coal, they spent their money at the coal owner's shops and lived in the coal owner's houses and they had it all sewn up, the money never really left the coal owner's pockets, it went round in a circle. And that was why the coal miners were so resentful of the coal mine owners and again, forming the Unions was to try and break that circle.

They used to have an allowance of coal; people used to say that they got free coal, yes, they did, but they used to have to dig it themselves, they used to have to load it in the sacks themselves and then they used to carry it from the mine, three miles back to the house and he had to do that when he was 13 years old, so yes, they got free coal but they had to work for it.

During the General Strike he [W.C. Rogers] went with a group of mining lads and made a choir and they used to go round to different venues and he found himself in Grimethorpe. After the General Strike was over he went to work in the Grimethorpe pit and he said he'd never had it so good as when he moved to there because he was actually standing up for the first time in his life, in a dignified manner, cutting coal. Normally they were down on their hands and knees.

William Cromwell Rogers, aged 13 – miner.

Accounts such as this are invaluable in giving readers an understanding the lives of their ancestors.

Social reformers can provide the family historian with material on working and social conditions. Friedrich Engels (1820–95), a German who was sent to Manchester by his father, became involved with the Chartist movement. He was shown the working conditions of the poor in Manchester and 'forsook the company and the dinner-parties, the port and champagne of the middle classes and devoted my leisure hours almost exclusively to intercourse with the plain Working Men; I am both glad and proud of having done so', subsequently writing *The Condition of the Working Class in England* in 1844. If you have ancestors who were miners in the middle to late nineteenth century, Engels's accounts of their experiences will be of particular interest since during the course of his research he conducted interviews with them. As well as miners, Engels also interviewed factory workers and the poor of Manchester, so if your ancestors lived and worked in Manchester in that period you will find the Engels' accounts of these interviews of particular value. Here is Engels recording what the miners told him:

> In the mines children of 4, 5 and 7 years are employed. They are set to transporting the ore or coal loosened by the miner from its place to the horse path or main shaft and to opening and shutting the doors. For watching the doors the smallest children are employed, who thus pass 12 hours daily in the dark, alone, sitting in damp passages.
>
> The transport of coal on the other hand is very hard labour, the stuff being shoved into large tubs without wheels, over the uneven floor of the mine, often over moist clay or through water, up steep inclines and through paths so low roofed that workers are forced to creep on hands and knees. For this more wearing labour, older children and half grown girls are employed ... two boys per tub, one pulls and the other pushes ...
>
> All the children and young people employed in hauling coal and ironstone complain of being overtired. Not even in a factory where the most intensive methods of securing output are employed do we find the worker driven to the same limits of physical endurance as they are in this assertion. It is a very common occurrence for children to come home from the mine so exhausted that they throw themselves on to the stone floor, fall asleep at once without being able to take a bite of food and have to be washed and put to bed while asleep; it even happens that they lie down on the way home and are found by their parents late at night asleep on the road. It seems to be a universal practice among these children to spend Sunday night in bed to recover in some degree from the over-exertion of the week.

Due to the poor conditions the miners worked in and the fact that they had been working in them since they were very young and still physically developing, many incurred a physical deformity such as curvature of the spine or bandy legs.

In the box on p. 36 you will find a list useful for locating contemporary accounts of other social reformers. Research will also allow you to give your readers an insight into the minutiae of your ancestors' daily lives, commenting on what their living conditions may have been, what they had in their kitchens, how much money they earned, what they ate and their beliefs and customs. This book will demonstrate that you cannot possibly write a family history without an appreciation of the times in which your ancestors lived and social history will provide you with enough material on these and other subjects related to your ancestors' lives to lend depth and interest to your story.

Social Reformers and Fields of Activity	
William Cobbett (1762–1835)	championed the cause of the agricultural labourer
Richard Cobden (1804–65) and John Bright (1811–89)	Anti-Corn Law movement and the principle of Free Trade
Elizabeth Fry (1780–1845)	prison reform and associated changes in legislation: Goals Act 1823
John Howard (1726–90)	primarily responsible for prison reform and associated changes in legislation: Goal Act 1774; published *The State of the Prisons in England and Wales* (1777)
Florence Nightingale (1820–1910)	hospital hygiene and nursing reform
Robert Owen (1771–1858)	founder of the Co-Operative movement and factory reform
Emmeline Pankhurst (1858–1928)	women's suffrage; representation of the People Act 1918; reforming workhouse conditions
Lord Shaftesbury (7th Earl, 1801–85)	set up 'ragged schools'; influential in passing of the Mining Act 1842
William Wilberforce (1759–1833)	significant influence on Abolition of Slavery Act 1833

You may wish to consider joining or contacting a local history group in your area or the one you are interested in concerning your relatives. These groups may be able to provide you with a wealth of knowledge, especially if you do not live near to where your ancestors did.

REFERENCE BOOKS

Whenever your ancestors lived, whatever they did and wherever they came from there will be a reference book or books that you can turn to to discover more information about them.

These are particularly useful for arming you with an understanding of your ancestors, maybe through researching a particular period in history, occupations or simply finding out more detail of their daily lives, often through the use of contemporary sources. It is always worthwhile to scan the bibliographies in books thoroughly for further material on a subject.

If, for example, your relative was involved in conflict or a war, anything you can find out about his (or her) unit, ship or regiment, the uniform worn, service life, pay rates and where he or she may have served and the actions participated in will bring these facts to life when you associate them with your relative.

It is also important to remember that if there is a particular subject you need information on your library should be able to help in finding it. If you have identified a source and the library does not have the book, if it is available in another county you should be able, for a small fee, to use the inter-library service to get it. Failing this, find a good bookshop with a search facility in order to locate the book you need, although ultimately this may involve you having to purchase the book once you locate it.

When searching for reference books, do not neglect to look in second-hand shops. If you find a good one it will carry stock on a wide range of subjects and, with luck, there may be a wealth of out-of-print material. The price charged for a book will reflect its scarcity value, but bargains are still to be found.

On-line book search websites are invaluable if you are trying to locate a work that is out of print.

Street Maps

The place your ancestors came from will undoubtedly have changed over the years, possibly substantially so. Portsmouth, for example, is now almost unrecognizable from its former appearance, with the exception of a few landmarks; in the early 1800s large parts of the present city were still under water and the districts that comprise it now were merely tiny villages and hamlets. To appreciate how a current large city was in the time when your ancestors would have lived there it is necessary to look at old maps.

Certainly if a town has been highly developed and you are struggling to find the street where your ancestors were born or the road they once lived in from census returns it may be worthwhile to obtain a copy of a contemporary street map. Your local library or record office should be able to help you find a map of the period you require. If the town or village is small, there may be a reprinted old Ordnance Survey map. I found for sale in a stationery shop in Shaftesbury a new copy of a 1901 street map of the town, which even had a small gazetteer including the surnames of inhabitants. The Ordnance Survey has a useful website through which copies of old maps may be purchased. These range in date from the mid 1800s to 1995.

Street and Trade Directories

Commercial and trade directories may also help you if your ancestors were in business. Street directories will help you to trace their movements if you know they resided in a particular town or city over some years. The chances are that they moved house frequently if they were in rented accommodation, and street

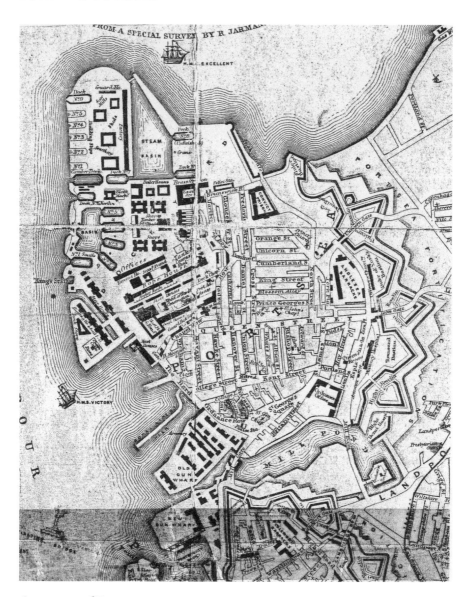

Street map of Portsea, 1866.

directories such as *Kelly's* or *White's* show street names, house numbers and the names of the occupiers.

INTERNET SOURCES

Assuming that you have access to a computer and the Internet – and, as it is now becoming more accessible through libraries and Internet cafes, this is a reasonable assumption – there are more sites for genealogy on the web than you can shake a stick at. In fact, next to pornography, it is the second most popular subject on the web.

The Internet is fast becoming the genealogist's most powerful tool for research purposes. More and more documents are being either transcribed or released into the public domain, especially through the National Archives. There are also many other projects under way to bring genealogical information to the Internet, such as those covering local and county family history societies. To keep up with the latest developments it may be advisable to buy one of the family history magazines which frequently update readers on forthcoming releases of information and documentation (there are also online family history magazines); this is by far the easiest way to keep abreast of new and useful websites.

There are books on the most useful websites relating to genealogy to aid you in your research, as well as more general information on history, on specific moments or events, and probably also on where your relatives were born and lived. I put into a search engine the name of the village of Evercreech, thinking that it was too tiny even to warrant a mention on the web. How wrong I was – up came a site with a picture of the church and a history of the village, as well as a treasure trove of genealogical information on births, marriages and deaths from parish records, from which I discovered the oldest generation of my family. The possibilities are clearly endless.

Newspaper Archives

Newspaper articles or announcements of birth, deaths and marriages are some things that many families have among their papers. I have at least three newspaper articles in my possession about family members: one was the account of my great-great grandfather's drowning and the subsequent inquest in 1908; another about my grandfather's reunion with his cousins in Scranton, in the USA in 1943; and a recent article in a local newspaper on funerals and, as a further example, the paper used my drowned great-great grandfather, showing his name, the arrangements that had been made and the cost of the ceremony (this information had been supplied by a local funeral director). All three provided me with information that I previously knew nothing about, so I would encourage you to pursue any likely press coverage describing your relatives and trace it through a local library.

If your ancestor was involved in a particular conflict and you know where and when, and especially if it was a significant event such as the evacuation from Dunkirk, you might search newspapers to get a report. As a good example, I knew that my grandfather's brother had been killed on the *Royal Oak* in 1939 at Scapa Flow. In the library I came across an interview with a survivor of the ship in the *Daily Telegraph*. He described how the ship was torpedoed, of its going down, of the men being thrown into the water and how he was surrounded by the bodies of his fellow sailors. This article was invaluable in recounting the events of that tragedy when my relative lost his life:

Survivors of the *Royal Oak* last night told the story of the sinking of the 29,150 tons British battleship by a submarine in Scapa Flow. Earlier, Mr Winston Churchill, First Lord of the Admiralty, in a statement in the House of Commons, said that the battleship was sunk at anchor at Scapa Flow. Three or four torpedoes, striking in quick succession, caused the ship to capsize and sink. Vincent Marchant, 18, of Doncaster, described how he was asleep in his hammock when the first explosion occurred. 'I ran to the upper deck to see what happened, there was a second explosion 20 minutes later followed by a third and then a fourth. By that time the ship was tilting and she was sinking rapidly. Remembering what happened on the *Courageous* and the lesson that taught us, I stripped myself of all my clothing and, tying my safety belt around my waist, dived into the water. Searchlights were playing over the surface and I could see hundreds of heads bobbing around. Great volumes of oil started to belch up to the surface. My eyes started to smart and the faces of all the men swimming in the water turned a greasy black. I was caught in a searchlight for several minutes and saw that two of my pals were swimming alongside me. Later, however, they had cramp and disappeared. A small boat passed near at hand with someone on board shouting for survivors. I 'ahoyed' but they evidently did not hear me and the boat disappeared into the darkness. I swam and swam for I don't know how long but I must have gone about a mile and a half when I felt the rock under me. I scarcely remember what happened after that. It was like a nightmare. I have just a vague recollection of climbing up the sheer face of a cliff about 20 or 30 feet high. Another figure was climbing behind me but he slipped and crashed among the rocks below. He must have been killed or drowned. I lay down on the top of the cliff and lost consciousness.

Another grandfather recounted to an American newspaper, *The Scrantonian*, on 29 November 1943 (a copy of which he must have brought home with him to show the family) his experiences in France with the British Expeditionary Force:

'I was one of the favored at Dunkirk. I was wounded and was placed aboard a Channel packet that had been converted into a hospital ship. I did not go through the agonies suffered by those on the beaches under artillery fire and attacks of dive bombers. But I did see them undergoing the terrific bombardments before our ship left.' Rogers expressed himself as highly pleased with the turn of events in the European Theater of War, 'When I was in France under attack of dive bombers and heavy artillery, my wife and six children were being bombed every night at home in Portsmouth, the site of a naval base,' he declared, 'Now we are giving the Nazis the same treatment.'

It was obviously interesting to read in his own words what his last days were like when fighting in the war and before he was medically discharged. Without this article this fact would have been unknown to me. It may also be useful to use newspaper extracts to set the scene as to what was news at a particular time in your relative's life; for example, what the issues were on the day he or she was born.

Portsmouth Evening News *reporting James Cass missing at sea. (Courtesy of* Portsmouth Evening News.)

Should you find any press articles, especially if they are from the original newspapers, transcribe them and store the originals in loose, plastic wallets, but not too tightly otherwise the ink will transfer to the plastic.

Another example provided me with valuable information when my great-great grandfather died by drowning in the Solent. Subsequent enquiries in the local paper revealed that, on the night he left in his boat, a violent storm had occurred which caused havoc across the south coast and even more for my unsuspecting relative, who ultimately lost his life. He was reported as missing at sea and for fourteen days the newspaper ran the story of the storm, his subsequent disappearance, of his body being found and of the inquest, which gave a dramatic account of his last known movements from fellow seamen and his employers (*see* box below).

Extracts from the *Portsmouth Evening News*, 1908

Friday, 4 September; Solent Wreck: Portsmouth Barge Lost – Two Men Missing – The Worst Feared

No doubt now remains as to the fate of the barge *Emerald*, belonging to Messrs Crampton and Co., coal merchants and shipping agents of Portsmouth. The wreck of the vessel has been located in the Solent and the fate of the two men who were on board is unfortunately considered no longer a matter of doubt either.

The *Emerald* left Portsmouth on Monday for Lymington, with a load of coal and ran into the gale. On Tuesday some boatmen on Southsea Beach found the hatches and a quantity of other gear thrown up by the rough sea on the beach. The hatches were identified as belonging to the missing vessel. A boat said to have been borne by the *Emerald* was also thrown up near Southsea Castle, and this too was identified. Moreover, the *Lorna Doone* and several other steamers reported having seen the mast of a small vessel protruding above the water near the Bramble Buoy.

Messrs. Crampton and Co. sent their tug *Empress* out to the spot on Thursday but she returned without being able to find the mast. Today, the *Empress* went out again and this time she found it, a mile or a mile and a quarter to the south-west of the East Bramble Buoy, in seven fathoms of water. It was the topmast of the *Emerald* and was just showing at dead low water. The skipper of the *Empress* had the topmast broken off, and brought it back to Portsmouth.

The coast has been searched both on the mainland and the Isle of Wight with a view to ascertaining the fate of the two men, Cass and Leggatt, who were on the *Emerald*, but so far without result. Cass is a married man, belonging to Landport and Leggatt, whose address is at Milton, was about to be married.

Wednesday, 9 September; Foundered Barge – Portsmouth Man's Fate – Body Recovered at Hayling

This morning a man's body was found floating in Langstone Harbour and secured by the Hayling ferryman, who landed it near the ferry house, Hayling

Island. The remains have since been identified as those of J. Cass, who formed one of the crew of the barge *Emerald*, belonging to Messrs. Crampton and Co., which was lost during the gale in the Solent last week.

Friday, 11 September; Two Portsmouth Victims – Both Bodies Recovered

Some evidence respecting the loss on Monday week of Messrs. Crampton's barge *Emerald* and two lives was given at the Portsmouth Coroner's Court today, when the inquiry into the death of James Cass, the barge skipper, was opened. Cass, whose age was sixty, lived at 33 Derby Road, Stamshaw and according to the evidence of his son, left on August 31st with a cargo of coal for Lymington in the barge *Emerald*. From that time, the witness had heard nothing of his father, though it was said that the position of the barge had been found. The body was much decomposed but the witness was sure of the identification. The recovery of the body was described by 1st Class Petty Officer Hutchinson, of HMS *Royal Arthur*, who when in charge of special service boat No.2 in Stoke's Bay on Thursday afternoon, saw the body floating face upwards. One boot was only partly unlaced and the other off. Hutchinson took the body to the *Barfleur* and afterwards conveyed it to Portsmouth Gunwharf. The inquiry was adjourned until Monday next.

Monday, 14 September; Verdict 'Accidentally Drowned'

The adjourned inquest on the body of James Cass, aged 60 years, the master of the barge *Emerald*, belonging to Messrs. Crampton and Co., coal merchants of Portsmouth, was resumed by the Borough Coroner (Mr. T.A. Bramsdon) at the Town Hall this afternoon. It had been adjourned from last Monday in order that further evidence might be called. Walter William Keen, clerk to Messrs. Crampton and Co., said that the deceased, who was master of the barge *Emerald*, left with a load of about 65 to 70 tons of coal for Lymington on Monday 31st August. Nothing was seen of the deceased afterwards until his body was washed ashore.

The deceased was a good sailor, and quite up to his work. When he left, the weather was splendid but after he had been out for some while it became very stormy. The body of the other man who was with the deceased on the barge had been picked up in Langstone Harbour, and a verdict of 'accidentally drowned' was returned at the inquest. The last person to see the deceased's barge was a mariner named Alfred Thomas New, who sailed from the Camber in the barge Eva at the same time the *Emerald* left. When the storm came on, New made for Cowes and anchored at Old Castle Point, opposite Cowes. In the morning, the *Emerald* either broke away from her anchorage or drew anchor and sailed away from Cowes. New then lost sight of the vessel in the storm. A verdict of 'accidentally drowned' was returned.

The newspaper coverage of the incident enabled me and my readers to imagine the scene as my great-great-grandfather left the harbour that day. I thought it worth reproducing the reports here to illustrate how they provide a wealth of detail, including both my great-great-grandfather's employer and an eyewitness who was able to give an account of his last hours. The coverage the story received, from the time the barge was missing to the eventual inquest, helps one to appreciate the impact this must have had on a tiny coastal community, where everyone knew everyone else.

I think that, at that time, there was more press attention to detail, probably due to the fact there was no television and so a graphic account needed to be given. The examples given here show how much information can be gleaned from newspaper sources.

OBITUARIES

These are particularly useful in giving you an insight into your relatives' lives, with information likely to have been given by a close relative. It may be worth your while scanning local newspapers around the time that a relative died to check whether his or her passing was mentioned. As may be seen below, it was not just the rich and famous who merited an obituary:

Death of an Old Inhabitant

Our obituary of this week again records the death of an aged inhabitant of Sowerby Bridge – Mrs Mary Whitehead, of Quarry-hill, widow of Mr Samuel Whitehead who formerly carried on business as a grocer. Mrs Whitehead was born at Bradshaw Head, but has spent most of her days at Sowerby Bridge. For about 20 years she was a member of the Wesleyan Methodist society, but, when increasing infirmities prevented her attending the Brow Chapel, she joined the Independents at West End. She was an earnest and thoroughly consistent Christian. For ten months she was confined to her bed and her death took place on Saturday from sheer old age. She was 84 years old and is survived by two daughters and a son. Her burial took place at West End Chapel, on Wednesday and was attended amongst others, by the Rev. Mr Laycock, incumbent of St George's.

The Halifax Courier, Saturday, 29 August 1874

3 PERSONAL SOURCES

FAMILY MEMORIES AND ANECDOTES

Adding the 'flesh' to the bones is what every family historian wishes to do and this may be easier than you think. Supposing you have just three generations: yourself, your parents and your grandparents.

There is a potential wealth of family information here and it is for you to extract it.

Oral History Tape Recording

One effective method of capturing family information is to tape-record the memories of people. Listening to your living relatives' memories will give you a window on a vanished world. Unfortunately for me, my maternal grandparents, who were born around the turn of the last century, had died before I realized the benefits of this method, but I was able to use it successfully to record their surviving siblings and also their children and learned something about my grandparents' childhood.

In the absence of these grandparents, I learned from my uncles of their earliest memories of family life:

> I can remember lying, whether I was in a cot or a pram, but I can remember being in an air raid shelter at the back of our house. I can remember the square of the entrance, I can remember my father standing in the entrance to the air raid shelter and he's shaking his fist up, he's in his shirt sleeves and a clear blue sky and what looks like to be a load of marks, figures of eight and rounds in the sky and he's saying, 'Go after them and get the bastards.' That must have been a dog fight. I could draw a picture of that today and that's how I remember it.

I cannot overemphasize the importance of getting a tape-recording project started and what dividends it pays when trying to put together a written family history. It could also help in adding some real dialogue to your story, rather than your having to remember who said what to whom, to relate a particular story or event.

Prepare Questions

When you are about to make a recording have questions already prepared that you wish to ask; start with simple things, for example:

- when were they born?
- where were they born?
- why they have their Christian name?
- what their earliest memory is?
- do they remember their grandparents?
- if so, can they describe their grandparents and their parents?
- what they remember about their wedding day?
- what do they remember of national events such as jubilees, state funerals and coronations?
- what was their favourite food and drink?
- what was their favourite song, film or play?

Such subjects may also act as triggers for their memories. I included a question about favourite food and drink since this may demonstrate something unexpected or quirky; for example, one of my grandmothers may have said 'a nice plate of chitterlings', and you would probably have to be of a comparable age to know that they were pigs' intestines. I venture to say that this does not appear on too many family menus today, which is precisely why it may be of interest. It may also be worth asking them about Christian names since they may have been named after a particular relative such as a grandmother, aunt or uncle, which will give you another, possibly hitherto unknown ancestor, or simply, as in the case of my great aunt Holly who was so called because she was born on Christmas Day.

There would have been some leisure time, however little, in our ancestors' lives and it is worth asking your relatives about how they spent it; and I think that it is interesting to demonstrate, when writing your history, if for no other reason, that they enjoyed far simpler pleasures than we seem to today.

If your family were anything like mine, the radio and the cinema seemed to play a large part in their lives. The radio was an important source of information as well as being a cheap source of entertainment. Ask them what their favourite radio programmes were since some of these can now be bought today copied on to tape or compact disk so that you could actually share in their experiences.

With television not coming widely into people's homes until the late 1950s, the cinema, as well as showing films, was also a source of information, and especially during the war years when newsreels provided the sense of actuality that we now get from television. Ask too about their favourite radio and film stars.

Band concerts and dance halls were where many people met their future husbands and wives, with the good dancers attracting the most attention. Ask your relatives to describe what the places were like, what the dances were called, what they danced to and what music they listened to.

What presents did your grandparents have for Christmas? Unless their families were well off, there is a good possibility that they looked forward to the same as mine:

> For Christmas we had an orange, an apple and a few nuts and a penny, that's all we had. No toys, my goodness me no. You know those silly wooden dolls with their arms sticking out, well we might have had one of them stuck in a stocking.

I cannot imagine this going down too well with any children I know!

Further Preparation
Preparation is the key for you to play family 'detective' in the gentlest possible way to elicit the information you want. Use photographs to jog memories and do not interview relatives alone unless they specifically so ask since another family member will not only keep them company but may stimulate them to remember more.

It is also worth noting that the sequence in which people tell you things or in which you ask questions will not be important. Rather than start with 'when were you born', you may wish to ask what their earliest memory was, which may lead quite naturally on, for example, to their grandparents. They key is to stimulate their memories and to let them talk on, rather than to ask only direct questions which may elicit only direct answers. By letting people talk as they wish they will gain in confidence and are more than likely then to give you answers to questions before you need to ask them.

Equipment Check
One last tip for preparation: check your equipment and do not do as I did when I turned up to interview my two elderly aunts. This was my second trip to see them, and I was so pleased with the outcome of our first session that I decided to upgrade my equipment and bought a new recorder. When I plugged it in and did a test to check that all our voices could be heard, there was nothing. It took me a while to realize that the machine had no internal microphone and that I needed an external one, which, of course, I did not have with me. Needless to say, the trip was very frustrating since they wanted to talk and did, with me hopelessly trying to remember the things they said.

Sensitive Subjects and Wartime Experiences
You will know those closest to you best and so you will also know whether you can ask some questions of a sensitive nature. Relatives who went through the Second World War may need to be treated carefully and sensitively if you want them to recount their experiences for you. I can remember as a 10- or 11-year- old child, having watched a war film in the presence of one of my grandfathers, turning excitedly to him and asking whether he had ever shot anyone in the war. I could not understand his apparent reluctance to answer. Luckily for me, one of my uncles had sat and listened to stories another

grandfather had told him and was able to recount some when I interviewed him about this relative:

> My father, during the war? He wouldn't speak about the war generally, but there were times when he would speak about it. They were guarding an airfield at a place in France and he had a mate who they used to call 'Shady Lane'. There was a song which prompted him to tell us the story and when he heard the song he started crying, and I said to him, 'What are you crying for?', and he said, 'I'll tell you a story.' Dad said he either owed his mate some money or he owed him. They were out in the open when these Germans attacked the airfield. My father ran one way and this fellow ran the other. My father went into the NAAFI place[1] which didn't get hit, and, just as his mate got to this other place, it got a direct hit and he was lying on a mound of dirt with his stomach hanging out and he was in agony. He said if he'd run with our dad he would have been alright, but he ran the other way. His name was Lane and they used to call him 'Shady' Lane and when the song came on, this used to get him stirred up.

It is interesting to note how this memory was triggered after my grandfather had heard a song, rather than his being directly questioned by my uncle. In another story he recounted the following memory:

> Dad was having a bath at the time in a trench. He'd nearly finished but his mate had already finished and dried when Jerry hit them. The gun was set up in the field so his mate ran for the gun, jumped on the gun, started popping away at Jerry, but Jerry hit him, direct hit and killed him stone dead. It was only lucky that dad was in the trench at the time having a bath or that could have been him.

Choosing Interviewees

Identifying Relatives

Any family members who are willing to participate and share their reminiscences with you are an asset, but you may also consider targeting those you think may have particular information. For example, you may have a particularly elderly relative with memories of more distant events. If you have not had any contact with them for some time or have yet to introduce yourself to them, do not delay but be honest about what you want to talk about.

I indicated earlier that my grandparents had died before I began to use this method, and so I recorded my grandmother's sisters, both in their late seventies at the time. I interviewed both together in the same room. They were willing to share with me their memories and knew the microphone was there. It quickly developed into a chat about 'the old times', rather than an interrogation. They also helped each other to remember things. It may be useful not to interview your relatives singly but be in the company of a son or daughter, especially if you are not well known to them.

It may also be worthwhile to choose less obvious candidates for family information, as well as those who may more obviously spring to mind. For example, I once interviewed a cousin of my great-grandfather. He was long deceased and this cousin was unknown to me until a chance introduction was made. Since she was 92 years old, I was not expecting to get much information, and certainly not in relation to my own family and was also prepared for poor recollection. I could not have been more wrong – Beatrice was a marvel, she had failing eyesight but her memory and recall were as still sharp and her slight deafness meant that she spoke loudly and clearly for the tape. Born in 1896, she was 10 years old at the time that my great-grandfather was trying to avoid marriage to my great-grandmother, and she remembered it all vividly. What gossip this was for me, and to hear all this 80 years on was nothing short of a miracle! She was also able to tell of a close, long-gone community where the family and extended family all lived near to each other, intermarried, knew what each other was up to and looked out for one another. In short, she was a mine of information. From my own experience, I cannot overstress the importance of identifying and choosing seemingly less promising interviewees.

There are a few things to remember when interviewing family members and especially the elderly ones:

- treat your relatives with the respect they deserve
- remember that they are not daft – just older than you are
- be patient and sensitive, and
- never forget that they are part of your family.

Family Gatherings

When a gathering is due – a wedding, birthday or a funeral – this may be a good opportunity to acquaint yourself with family members and to let them know of your intentions. I interviewed my maternal grandfather's brother at a party for his 80th birthday. This was somewhat remarkable in that he had suffered a stroke in the past and had recovered well; he was able to tell me about his father and childhood with his brothers.

Funerals, although generally sad occasions, may involve a wake and this can have relatives reminiscing and telling stories of dare doings – remember to listen, and, if you think that you may get away without upsetting anyone, take along a hand-held recorder. The funeral of one of my grandfathers ended with a 'knees-up' which included the vicar, who, having arrived on his bicycle, then had to be driven home because, at the end, he was rather the worse for wear, a less gloomy event would be hard to imagine, with lots of reminiscing but, unfortunately, no tape recorder.

Transcribing Tapes

Once you have your precious tape recordings, these people become your eyewitnesses to past events – yours and your readers' eyes to the past.

What do you do now that you have your tape of your uncle talking about the Second World War? – transcribe it. Write it out, type it out or preferably put it into a computer, either adding in your questions or leaving them out and writing a long script, as if your interviewee was telling a story. How much you transcribe is up to you – if it was all riveting to hear then you may like to keep it all or only parts. I had to make an abridged transcript of my paternal grandmother's tape simply because she swore so much in it, I could not subject any reader to an unabridged version.

Using the Transcript
Once transcribed you and your readers should find this a fascinating insight into how people used to live. It could elicit some gems of family gossip, information about the past and people. Some of mine retell events that are reminiscent of the Ealing film comedies, stories that are all the better for coming from the mouths of the participants, rather than trying to tell them yourself:

> When they had the Coronation, they used her (my great-grandmother) store to make all the street bunting and that, and then Uncle Ray got a ladder and rigged up the lights and plugged into the street lamp and they had all the lights and electric free for about a week, while they were celebrating.

> I used to work round British Engineering Productions. The boss there was so tight! One day he said, 'We've got to get this order out, don't matter what time we work to, I'll pay you.' There was a man there called Eric, and I said to him that all we had to do was get as much done through the day as we could so we wouldn't have to stay until 11 o'clock that night. 'Alright', he said, 'but what about clocking off? He'll know what time we left.' I said, 'We could put the clocking-off machine in a sack and take it home.' So that's what we did. So there was I, on the back of his motorcycle with the clock in a sack, a sandbag, and I got home and put it next to my bed, and as I lay in bed, I clocked everyone out at 11 o'clock. This worked well and went on for the rest of the week until one morning I could hear Eric's bike coming down the road early and he said, 'The boss is coming in early this morning, we've got to get the clock back before he comes in.' So off we go with the clock in the sandbag. When we got to work, the clock wouldn't come out of the bag, so we locked the door to the factory while we wrestled with the clock, but we got it back in and the boss was none the wiser! The things we got up to.

As they say, a good anecdote is in the telling. A great aunt of mine recounted an early memory of her teenage years:

> My stepfather died of pneumonia. He had a false leg when Mum married him, Mum said he was kicked by a horse. Well, after he died, Mum put his leg in a cupboard, up in her bedroom, and it was always full of clothes this cupboard. The baby's cot was

in front of the cupboard, and every time I went to the cupboard, the leg fell out, so when Mum was out one day and I never had anything to burn up for the copper when I needed some hot water, I thought, I know, I'll put that leg in. I never thought any more of it, I never said anything to Mum, I didn't think she'd even think about it. It must have been a year or more later and one day, Mum went to the cupboard for something and she said, 'Here Hol, what became of your father's leg?' I said, 'I put it up the copper, Mum a long time ago.' 'Oh my god, how could you do that?', she said. I said, 'Well, Mum, it wasn't any good, you couldn't sell it could you?' You'd have thought I'd done the worst crime out because I stuck his leg in the copper. I've laughed to myself since, because, instead of putting the foot part of it in first, I stuck the part with the metal bits at the side first, and it wouldn't burn and the foot was hanging out, and I had to keep getting something to poke the foot up!

Once you have made your transcript you could use it in its entirety within your story and include photographs of the person being interviewed to illustrate it. In this way your transcript can help you to construct your written family history. When using purely factual information you can blend it with your transcripts to personalize events. This is an extract from one of my own family histories dealing with the loss of the *Royal Oak* that has already featured in this book:

At the start of the war in October 1939, Leading Seaman Leonard Cass P/JX 132259 found himself aboard the battleship HMS *Royal Oak* off the Scottish coast at Scapa Flow, the base of the fleet. His sister, Nellie Cass Prior, spoke of her brother: 'Leonard never married. He would have been 27 in the November as he got killed on the 14th October. The war started in 1939 and he was on the boat when they took it up to Scotland to get out of the way, because he was going to Malta for two years. He said, "Don't worry, I shan't be there all that long." He was going up there to get his stripes and the bloody German submarine got in and got it. The ship's still up there; they say that when the tide is in you can see it, but they won't bring it up.' On the 14th October 1939 the *Royal Oak* was torpedoed by German submarine U-47 led by Lieutenant-Commander Gunther Prien with the loss of 810 crew, including Leonard.

How you use the transcript is a matter of choice, whether you use direct quotations from them or précis them to use in among factual material to personalize it, without detracting from it. I use a combination of both, as above, to make the story both gossipy and more generally anecdotal.

I also keep my family history transcripts in a separate section as I think the readers should be provided with the whole text to read if they wish (*see* Creating Supplements and Appendices in Chapter 5).

Finally as to the tape itself: my grandmother was a something of a matriarch and, although I taped her long before her death, I copied the tape for other members of the family to listen to while she was alive. Now that she is dead, a cousin recently said how she would play the tape regularly since hearing my grandmother's recollections cheered her up.

FAMILY PHOTOGRAPHS

There's nothing like seeing a photograph of an ancestor, putting a face to a name and comparing likenesses with other relatives. Do you wish you that had a picture of your great-grandfather? Never give up on finding one. Speak to relatives since this may unearth many a photograph of someone you may have had no hope of ever seeing – after 25 years of research a photograph of my great-grandfather, then aged 32, suddenly surfaced from a cousin of my father. A good tip: do not neglect parents' cousins – bear in mind that cousins of your parents will also have had a share in your grandparent's lives and therefore in photographs and memories of them.

Every picture tells a story, so they say. If there is a photograph of a relative that intrigues you, try to find out the story behind it. If there is one of a family gathering, try to find out what the occasion was since this will provide you with another story complemented by its own illustration. Remember to use photographs when interviewing relatives to jog their memories or to prompt them to remember an event.

Examine your photographs carefully since they may not be all that they seem. In the accompanying illustration at face value it is a photograph of the family of William and Elizabeth Carhart, taken during the First World War. If you look more closely you will see that the image of William has been superimposed since he was not actually present when it was taken, but Elizabeth wanted a photograph of her family altogether; William was away fighting in the war.

Elizabeth Carhart and her nine children, taken during the First World War; William Carhart has been superimposed in the photograph.

Do not neglect to look on the backs of photographs for names and dates. My grandmother would write messages and shopping lists on the backs of any pictures that happened to come to hand at the time. On the back of a photograph of her sister-in-law, obviously not long after giving birth to her last child, she wrote her list of things to do and to buy for the day:

> Baby flannel
> 1 Bottle of milk of magnesia
> 1 small modern tit
> Register Baby – Janet Jean
> Hand in Ration Book – get new one.

If you cannot decide on which photographs to include and which to leave out of your history, or there are many photographs of one or more particular relatives, you may wish to consider creating a gallery of photographs within your story. This will be easily done if you have a computer and scanning equipment.

Originals

Always treat original photographs with care. The best way of preserving the images is to take a copy of them or to scan them into a computer. Scanning your photographs will mean that they are easily transferable to your document if you compile your history by using a computer. If the photographs are damaged or faded, with the right software you can tidy them up, restore them and enhance the images.

PICTURE POSTCARDS

When considering photographic material do not neglect old picture postcards – which are still reasonably priced – and from which you may find an old view of the town or village your relatives came from. These could form an attractive addition to your story, to show a place as your relatives might have known it.

Picture postcards are particularly useful if you have a limited number of family photographs since they can be used to set a scene. Your first port of call might be the Francis Frith Archive which holds 365,000 photographs of 7,000 towns and villages taken from 1860 to 1970, some by the pioneering Frith himself and a team of photographers. If you find what you are looking for it is possible to order a print from the website. If you are unsuccessful here, then try local flea markets and antique fairs for specialist dealers in picture postcards.

Specialist Subjects

If you decide to add picture postcards to your story consider also looking at more specialist subjects. For example, if an ancestor was a blacksmith look out for a postcard of one or of a smithy since this would give you and your readers a good idea of his working environment. This is especially useful for occupations which now have few practitioners.

Postcard showing Shaftesbury in Dorset, in about 1900.

Postcard showing miners in a coal mine.

DIARIES

If any of your relatives wrote a diary you may wish to use it to give your story a particular boost. Some people are avid diary keepers and so, while you may not wish to use all of the available material, well-chosen extracts will give depth and poignancy to your story. By transcribing the diary the original can be left intact without any need to refer to it subsequently and thereby render it fragile as time goes on.

In researching my own family history, I happened upon a distant cousin in Australia whose family emigrated there in 1862. Our stories connected back to the 1700s with two brothers, one of whom was a many-times great-grandfather of mine and the other whose grandson had emigrated. My newly-found cousin was already an avid family historian and, luckily for me, had much material that he was willing to share. Among the items he sent to me was an extract from the diary our ancestor had kept on board the ship carrying him and his family to Australia. Joseph Ingamells, a schoolmaster, and his family boarded the 1,244-ton *The Prince of Wales* at London on 5 July 1862. It then stopped at Plymouth on 14 July, where more passengers embarked, before sailing to Melbourne.

In the accompanying box a selection of the diary entries is reproduced which give a good insight into life on board ship at this time and are probably fairly typical of early immigrants' experiences (*see* Chapter 4).

The Diary of Joseph Ingamells on *The Prince of Wales*

Plymouth, Wednesday 16th July 1862 – Sailed this morning at half past 6 o'clock – a strong breeze all day – but not very favourable. Tacking all day – little progress. Many who came on board at Plymouth have been sea-sick – a few also of those who sailed from London, Mrs I among the rest. We shall be some time getting clear of land unless the wind changes – the breeze we now have would drive us rapidly if a fair one.

Thursday July 17th 1862 – Very strong wind – cold – dull- rainy. The sea literally boiling like a pot or cauldron. Sailing rather fast but not exactly right direction – about 50 miles S.W. from the Scilly Isles. Many sick partly on account of the ship's violent motion, and partly on account of having all the portholes closed, making the intermediate department smell very close and foul. Very few able to be on deck. I put on my oil jacket that I bought at Plymouth and walked or rather staggered about on deck, not without enjoying the scene though ship dipped considerably first one end, then the other – not the slightest danger however apparently – the chief mate tells me I may expect to see it much worse that this.

The Diary of Joseph Ingamells on *The Prince of Wales* continued

Monday 21st July – Lat 45-52 Long 8-10. A beautiful day. Very little wind, very slow sailing. Feel we are getting into warmer weather, passengers putting on lighter clothing.

Tuesday 22nd July – Lat 44-58. Long 8-13. Not much wind, but fair, hence our progress better. A pleasant cool day. An awning up to keep off the sun's rays. Provisions: All pretty good, excepting tea, plenty of it but poor quality. We mix a little of our good green among it and that means get a very fair cup. We require

to be very sparing with our water to make it hold out. Our supply of animal food is much too great, the children eat so little of it. I tried to get more flour and less meat but could not succeed. The authorities are very respectful but said that they had laid in their ship's stores in proportion to our rations, therefore could not alter. We may therefore have probably flour to buy. The children cannot eat the biscuits. We can sympathise with them as we cannot eat them ourselves, at least not many of them. I am afraid we may be teased with rats. We have divided our bag of flour into about 6 little lots and hung them from the beams in our berth, by this means we hope to keep clear of the mischievous fellows. The authorities have taken up the rice and raisins from the hold as the black thieves had made a bold start upon them – the rest of the provisions are in strong wooden casks. I fear they will be the more inclined to come up out of the hold into our berth as their food is taken from them. One young man of a company of 8 is much afraid of them, and the other 4 last night kept him awake about an hour seeking rats by scratching – making noises – one of them contrived to get his hairy slipper pushed into bed to him, of course, the poor fellow took it for a rat and was quickly out of bed, and there they kept him light in hand a long time though no rat was near and they were not a little merry over it. Our merry fellow last night dressed in female clothes and walking into the berth of a modest young man (a baptist). The baptist said, my good woman, you are in the wrong berth, but the mock-female instead of walking off would have a kiss. The baptist's modesty of course was not a little shocked as he took the merryman for a female. Another merry fellow made a sham boy with a blanket rolled up, he put it into the baptist's bed to represent the baptist's brother. When the young fellow entered his cabin, he shouted, Chris, Chris, are you asleep? (the boy's name is Christopher). Hence, you see we have a few merry fellows to keep us from being over sober.

Wednesday 6th August – Last night very squally, teeming showers and strong wind, no danger. Hatched down several times to keep out the rain, very much sickness in the morning owning to the confined air more than the heat, though the latter was great. A young gentleman, a first class passenger, brother of the doctor, who as it appears served an apprenticeship at sea, was at the time of a squall running up the mast by the side of a sailor trying to be first, when very high he lost his hold and fell to the deck and in a short time was corpse.

HOBBIES

Do not neglect to find out about your ancestor's hobbies. This could uncover stories and lead to more material for your story. In the 1930s and the 1940s, one of my grandfathers was known as a very good snooker player and won many cups and shields (all sacrificed to the pawn shop when times were hard). This was at a time before snooker became commercial and was televised, and my uncles remain convinced that, had my grandfather been born at a different time, he would have been good enough for national recognition. As it was, while he was away in Bermuda during the war years, working on a floating dry-dock project, he must have utilized his skills well:

> When dad was doing his American bit, during the questioning from either the *New York Times* or *New York Post*, he happened to tell them that he was good at snooker and billiards and, of course, they love competition, the Yanks, and somebody picked it up and they put him in touch with a fellow in Bermuda, he wasn't an exiled gangster but I mean, he was a gangster *per se*, but he had a big house on Bermuda. Dad said it was all done out in pink. And he was a gangster and, of course, they used to have the 'hustler' bit in them days and he wanted our dad to play his man, you know. I suppose the old man probably backed himself, beat the other man and got the money! Dockyard wages wouldn't allow him to save hundreds of pounds so I can only assume he won it. He definitely played at a gangster's house anyway, in Bermuda.

My parents are avid collectors – my father of vinyl long-playing records, with a collection of 3,000 recordings of assorted artists, and my mother of teapots, with approximately sixty on display in the kitchen on a high shelf. Tell your readers of any collecting hobbies by relatives, and ask relatives whether they like to collect anything and what may have started them off in the first place. Descriptions of collections could be of interest to future readers, with today's collections becoming tomorrow's antiques.

PERSONAL CORRESPONDENCE

Letters from relatives are highly personal effects which will convey to you direct their thoughts and feelings. It is therefore worth remembering this if you are given or find any personal correspondence, since the writer most probably intended the content to be read only by the recipient. If you are lucky enough to have personal correspondence from a relative that is useful for your history, first transcribe it and use only the relevant parts in your story, although you could include copies of the entire originals in your history as addenda. Correspondence is sometimes in illegible handwriting and on thin paper, and so taking the time to transcribe it will be a safeguard against possible loss, save your readers from the risk of misreading it and also preserve the original.

Letters to family members provide an insight into family life and often some surprises. In a letter to his grandson, my great-grandfather revealed how he had once cycled from Wales to London to watch cricket for a day when he was 44:

> I went up to see Australia and M.C.C. at Lords in 1921 and rode all the way there and back by push bike. The Aussies were too good for us that time, I only stayed one day, but would have stayed longer if I had had company, fancy feeling lonely in London.

Correspondence that is written regularly, even daily, for example, if a relative was in the Services and written to by his wife or mother, will provide you with much detail about his life. I have a good deal of the correspondence between my parents before they married, when my father was overseas in the early 1960s. The minutiae of their daily lives is all the more fascinating for the lack of reference to distractions such as television programmes and gives a good insight into life then.

POSSESSIONS AND GIFTS

Mention in your family history any particular possessions of your relatives that you have or know of. These could include musical instruments, pictures, jewellery, furniture or books. Family heirlooms often have a history of their own and so do not neglect to ask for any stories relating to items such as wedding rings, pocket watches and christening gowns. Drawings and paintings either owned or created by a relative will enrich your family story; remember that behind each treasured possession lies a story, half the charm of televised antiques programmes is listening to how people came by their possessions.

A wedding ring especially is likely to be passed on to another family member on the death of a relative. I know that my brother was particularly close to my paternal grandmother and gave his wife my grandmother's ring when they married, which is an appealing and particularly sentimental way of adding continuity and of linking the generations of the same family. Wedding rings may also provide other stories – my own ring has been used twice, once for my own wedding and again for that of my brother-in-law and sister-in-law when the rings were temporarily mislaid.

Medals are likely to have particular significance for their former owners and are especially worthy of note in your history since they will tell of an involvement in war and could give you more fruitful avenues for research.

VIDEO RECORDINGS AND HOME MOVIES

We have spoken of family gatherings and what better way of capturing relatives for future generations than by cine-film or video tape?

While obviously you cannot use these direct in your story, you can refer your readers to them; for example, you could say that on Video number 2, showing June and Phillip's wedding at St. Mary's Church on whatever date it was, the family is shown arriving at the church. You could then go on to describe and identify old family members, especially if they are now long since dead, by the clothes they wore, or where they were standing in relation to other family members. While you may take knowing who these people were for granted, a generation or two to come will be fascinated by seeing their relatives thus preserved and thank you for having taken the trouble to point out who was who, rather than their having to guess.

My father is an amateur Cecil B. de Mille and in the early 1960s he attended family weddings with his cine-camera, filming his brothers' weddings, with the attending grandparents, parents, aunts and uncles. When we look at these films now it is pure nostalgia – the way everyone seemed to smile so self-consciously as soon as they were on camera, the vivid clothes colours and the recognition of those now long gone. Whenever I watch these I am left wanting more – they never seem to stay focused on any one person for long, the films themselves are never long enough and over too soon.

Technological advances now mean that these cine-films can be transferred to video tape and to more durable compact disks, so it is advisable not to neglect this method of preservation.

THE MASS-OBSERVATION ARCHIVE

In 1937 three young men founded Mass-Observation in order to study the lives of ordinary people; they felt that at that time little was known about them and wished to find out more and in their own words. To do this they recruited a team of observers and a panel of volunteer writers. In describing their first year's work in 1938 they wrote '... we are continually impressed by the discrepancy between what is supposed to happen and what does happen, between law and fact, the institution and the individual, what people say they do and what they actually do, what leaders think people want and what people do want.'

The Archive went to Sussex University in 1970 and you can discover more about the Archive from their website (see Further Information). It is still active and now has no fewer than 250 contributors, with recruitment drives taking place often. Contributors are asked for their thoughts and feelings about particular subjects and, through their contributions, a snapshot of the country's attitudes emerges. There is a standard thirty-year embargo on the release of personal details and writings. Contributors also need to have given permission for their writing to be seen by members of their families, but it would be worth considering if you know that a relative had written for Mass-Observation. It would give a wonderful insight of their feelings at a particular time on once current events.

VISITING ANCESTRAL PLACES

It could be helpful to you if you were able to visit the places where your ancestors lived and worked. Even with the passing of several generations it is an easy way that you can still pick up interesting facts about their lives.

For example, on one trip to South Wales I went to visit a town graveyard on the off chance that a gravestone of my great-grandmother may have survived. It was a hot, sunny day, there were sheep grazing in the graveyard (a novel way to keep it tidy) and there were workers busy around a small, old chapel-like building. This was not a particularly well-kept place and, perhaps for this reason, I was able to make the discovery I did. I had my parents, aunt and uncle with me at this time and we started to look on the graves. From one of the workmen, my mother found that there was a 'book' in the building that they were storing their tools in. I took a look at the book with one of the workmen, and in it, a little ahead of the date on which we knew that my great-grandmother had died, we found an entry. We knew that she died in 1908, aged 28, from breast cancer, leaving a husband and three sons. What was also written under the entry was the fact that, twelve days later, her twelve-day old daughter Elizabeth was also buried with her. This fact came as a shock to my mother and aunt since they had always known about the tragic death of their grandmother so young, but not that she was also pregnant during her illness. The men were also able to take us to the grave – the stone, if there had been one, was no longer there, but they were able to point us to the site. To find a gravestone as well would have been especially rewarding, but we had discovered another relative we previously knew nothing about. If we had not made the journey we probably would never have learned of the brief and tragic existence of twelve-day-old Elizabeth.

On other trips I have discovered streets and houses where my ancestors lived and died. On a second trip to Wales we trudged up the steep road on which my great grandfather lived and stood outside what had been his house. The next-door neighbour came out and from her we discovered that she had lived there for fifty years and remembered my great-grandfather. Incredibly, she was able to recall him, his third wife and the fact that he would sing hymns when tending his garden.

To visit where your ancestors lived brings you closer to them – you can walk down the same streets, probably see the same buildings and views as they did, and if you go to the church where they were either christened or married you will know that they crossed the threshold for sure.

If you visit your ancestors' home town, try to make time to go to the local library which should be able to help with local history books, also look out for stationers shops or newsagents for local history books and street maps – I made finds in both that were not available in the library or the tourist information centre. Sites of historical interest in the area may also hold useful sources of local history information.

Plan Your Trip

Whether the journey to your forebears' home involves a few hours or days of travel, and especially if you come from overseas, do research and plan your visit as thoroughly as you can so that you do not have a wasted journey but use your time well. If your time is limited it may be useful for your research to find out whether the town has a local historical society that may be able to help when you have returned home.

If you have internet access use it to help you plan your visit. Many cities, towns and villages now have a dedicated website, and although some will be more sophisticated than others in layout they should provide you at the least with a street map and details of the major places of interest.

Before you go it will be useful to you to:

- Locate the tourist information centre (who should be able to provide a street map if you do not have internet access). You could also telephone for advice on parking and on accommodation if you planned to stay in the area for some time.
- Locate the local library; an advance call to them may save time in locating local history books and discovering the existence of any local history societies.
- If your time in the area will permit it, find a good place to eat; some websites recommend hotels, restaurants and pubs and give an idea of what to expect and of prices.
- If possible, explore local museums in advance via the Internet or telephone to see whether what they have may be of interest to you, and to establish opening hours.

If your visit is limited to a few hours, try to avoid any local archives, unless you have specifically travelled to see them. With the best will in the world, if you make a visit to a local archive intending to spend just an hour or two wading through census returns or parish registers and use the rest of the time visiting the places you have earmarked, the chances are that these documents will totally absorb you and your precious time. Local archives can be wonderful but they are likely to need a special trip to consult them; if you can afford it, pay someone to look at them for you to save you the trip.

[1] *Navy, Army, and Air Force Institutes; an organization providing service canteens and other facilities in Britain and abroad.*

4 MAKING THE MOST OF LIMITED MATERIAL

What if you have only limited knowledge of the lives of your ancestors – can you still write a family history? The answer is yes, although to do so will still require some research. In this chapter we shall explore how you can still write about the life of your ancestor with scant information. You can also use it to make sure that you are making the most of the information that you do have.

Suppose that you are researching a dead ancestor and all you have are the bare facts of his or her birth, death and marriage. There are no possessions, no photographs, no anecdotal information, only the bare, minimal facts contained on these certificates for you to reconstruct a life with. Nevertheless, a study of them alone will provide you much material. With just these three certificates and no other knowledge you will be able to inform your readers of the following facts about a particular relative:

Where your ancestor was born	*place of birth*
	geographical location
	the history of the place of birth
	location of the street and house
	time and date
	any significant dates or the time of year
His or her name	*whether a much-used family name*
Sex	*social distinctions between the sexes at the time the relative was born*
Names of parents	*mother's maiden name*
Status of parents	*married or widowed (a birth may be an indication of a recent marriage)*
Occupation(s) of the parents	*whether the occupations changed from when they married to when the relative was born*
Whom the relative married	*where they lived*

When your ancestor died	*the spouse's parents* *their parents' occupations* *who was present when the relative died* *cause of death* *place of death* *relative's occupation at time of death*

Each point above should provide you with material to enable you to comment on your ancestor's life. If you can cover all those in the list, you will have written about your ancestor quite fully by the time of his or her death.

RESEARCH ON LIMITED FACTS

This example can be followed if you have documentary evidence of the life of your ancestor. But what if you are really struggling, if you simply find you have no further factual information about your ancestor? There is still material you can add. For example, the earliest ancestor I can find on one side of my family is Ann Cass who had an illegitimate son Charles Cass. All I know of Ann is from one line in the parish register: 'Charles Cass baptised 21st August 1814 illegitimate son of Ann Cass, labourer.' A few years earlier, a daughter Martha is mentioned in the parish register, describing her as 'base born'. Apart from these two baptisms of her children, I can find nothing more about Ann and the only things I know are that she was Charles's and Martha's mother, she was unmarried and she was a labourer. I could find no evidence of her baptism nor any subsequent marriage, nor, indeed, of her death.

In a second-hand bookshop I found a book on women workers in the industrial revolution and from this information I was able to describe the plight of the agricultural woman labourer and thereby most probably describe the life of Ann Cass. I then went on to describe the small rural town of Shaftesbury where she lived and speculated on what farm she may have worked on and the nature of her work. Given the fact that her son was illegitimate, I could also speculate on the circumstances of his conception: was it that she was let down by her first love, had she fallen prey to one of her employers, had she been part of the gang system of labourers who were treated badly by the men who controlled them, or had she given into some farmer? Or was my ancestor's conception more deliberate? Although there was nothing more factual about Ann that I could find apart from the entry above, I gave her a presence in my family's story by offering an insight into what her life was probably like:

> Single unemployed women at this time found themselves in a situation whereby premarital pregnancy was their only means of escape from the pittance given to them by the parish. Once pregnant, the parish either provided the women with a husband or gave an increased allowance for her child. In either case she would be better off financially. The increase in illegitimacy was therefore deliberate, and

63

due far more to economic necessity and the hope of obtaining better maintenance and a home than to a lowering of moral standards.

Maybe this was the situation Ann found herself to be in.Whilst I do not know exactly where Ann lived in Shaftesbury, we do know at this time she worked for a living to help keep herself and her children. Chances are she lived either in a tied cottage or similar premises supplied by the parish. As labourers, women were employed in back-breaking work by farmers, who soon discovered that women and children could be successfully employed in those jobs which men were loath to do, such as weeding and turnip digging. Because men saw vegetable digging as demeaning work, it was often carried out half-heartedly so farmers more than welcomed women on to their farms. As a result, these jobs were often done more thoroughly by women who were grateful for the work and the chance to earn however little money was on offer. As for the farmers, not only could they get better work from women, but they could also exploit them by not paying them as much as they would have had to pay men to do the same job. It is likely, therefore, that Ann was employed as a 'day labourer' on one of the many farms and farmsteads that surrounded Shaftesbury at the time. It is also likely that this is where she met the father(s) of her children.

Film and Documentary References

I also referred my readers to the literature of Thomas Hardy who set his novels in and around nineteenth-century Dorset and chronicled the lives of people living in the rural towns and villages. *Tess of the d'Urbevilles* is set in Shaftesbury, shows an intimate knowledge of the town and follows the downfall of Tess Durbeyfield. I mentioned to my readers the film of the book, and while Ann Cass's experiences were obviously very real, the film *Tess* (1980) shows her plight as a poor agricultural worker fallen on hard times, working in all weathers. To give my readers a visual realization of how Ann Cass might have worked and its probable nature, this does rather well.

If you think that to compare your relatives' lives with Hollywood films is rather fanciful, let me tell you of my great-grandfather's comparison of his own experiences to those depicted in the cinema. In a letter that he wrote to his grandson he makes mention of the film *How Green Was My Valley* (1941) which shows a mining community. He says that, 'it was very good, but to an old miner who knows, the falling debris in the mine was very overdone', and how he thought the exaggerated size of the firing box 'very funny'! His reference to the film and the fact that he thought it was good, despite the exaggeration in the action scenes, I think lends a certain legitimacy to your directing your readers to filmic 'reproductions' of social history. Unfortunately, I do not know whether my great-grandfather ever read the book *How Green Was My Valley* by Richard Llewellyn to know whether the author's descriptions of family life in the South Wales mining area in the latter part of the nineteenth century were accurate. As another example, anyone involved in the D-Day landings in 1944 will almost certainly know of the films *The Longest Day* and *Saving Private Ryan* which give as realistic accounts of the landings as any re-enactment could (although the latter deals exclusively with the American involvement). For younger readers they would serve as the nearest idea they are likely to get of what it was like to have been there.

OTHER KEY AREAS FOR RESEARCH

Another way in which you can tell the story of your ancestors if you have no information of substance about them to expand upon is to tell your readers of the lifestyle they were likely to have led. For example, the following subjects could help you to outline an ancestor's life:

*   occupations
*   hearth and home
*   relationships
*   health and wealth
*   crime and punishment
*   emigration and migration.

In the following sections I shall expand on these to give examples of how, with limited material of your ancestors' lives, you can still give your readers a sense of how they probably lived.

OCCUPATIONS

All our ancestors had an occupation of some sort, from being a pauper (yes, even this was stated as an occupation on the census returns and birth, death and marriage certificates) to the more eminent positions of doctor or lawyer.

Without the benefit of the modern welfare system, without any means of earning a living, our ancestors had no way of surviving – the ultimate degradation being to be forced to turn to the parish and to incarceration in the workhouse. The workhouse was to be avoided at all costs, and from my own experiences of listening to grandparents and great-grandparents, some, although poor, were nevertheless far too proud to turn to the parish and would do literally anything rather than receive charity (*see* the Use of Literature and Poetry on p.85). What your ancestors did for a living would also define them in the social order and, unless they were very lucky, the chances are that they worked hard and for long hours for their wage.

An ancestor's occupation or trade should provide you with abundant research. They may have had an occupation that, although now rare, was once a quite common, everyday job just a hundred years ago, as for example, chimney sweep, wheelwright, blacksmith, carter, cobbler, glover or silk weaver. If your ancestor's occupation was one of those, a little research in your library or on the internet should provide enough information for you to inform your readers of their daily routine and what tasks they would have undertaken. Anything from the list above might be considered as unexciting today, but it could be that it is in fact the absence of computers and other contemporary marvels that makes our ancestors' lives so interesting.

Take, for example, the glover. Almost everyone wore gloves as a stock item of clothing up until around the middle of the twentieth century. There were riding gloves, evening gloves, working gloves, gloves for handling firewood and the cotton gloves worn by domestics; ladies and gentlemen never ventured out without them, almost everyone wore them. The glove itself also gave rise to accoutrements in the form of glove stretchers and button holers. Certainly in the middle of the eighteenth century there was a huge cottage industry in glove making. While the trade was not wholly confined to women, families could subsidize their incomes by setting their youngest daughters to work with needle and silk thread, sewing fine kid gloves for the hands of gentlemen and ladies. Men also worked in the glove-making trade by tanning, staining and cutting the skins. From the main centres at Yeovil, Leominster, Ludlow, Worcester, Woodstock and Hereford, the pieces were distributed throughout the many surrounding villages. Wages depended on speed and efficiency so rarely did one person complete a whole glove. Some would sew only the backs, some would sew only their sides, and each subsequent required piece would be passed on to someone else to finish. The early nineteenth century saw a decline in demand through the importing of cheaper and finer French products and many workers were forced to turn to the parish. After a subsequent return to the production of quality gloves, there was a revival in the industry and gradually the levels of employment improved. It took time for the use of sewing machines to spread and so the industry survived for decades into the nineteenth century. The hours worked were from 6 a.m. or daybreak until 10 p.m., and, of course, the longer the hours, the more was earned. The demand for gloves meant that children as young as 6 could earn a few pennies at home and thereby contribute to the family finances. Ancestors of mine aged 10 and 12 were employed in the trade and relatively simple research gave me, and thus my readers, a fascinating insight into the work they carried out.

Service in the Armed Forces

If your ancestor was in the Army, the Royal Navy or the Royal Air Force you might want to highlight his or her career in the Services.

Ask around your family and, most importantly, your extended family, for any career records your relative may have had. On a branch of my family with only relatively limited family documentation, I was lucky enough to have been given, by my uncle, my grandfather's Army Service Book. Through this I was able to tell my readers of his posting in India between 1929 and 1934, to serve in the North-West Frontier Province, which included the Khyber Pass, a 33-mile (53km) long route through the mountain range that separates what we now know as Pakistan from Afghanistan. I was also able to establish that he was sent to France in 1939 as part of the British Expeditionary Force (BEF) and rescued injured from Dunkirk aboard a converted liner hospital ship. I was able to glean all these facts from his small, red Service Book, which also gave a personal description of him and a glowing reference on his discharge. This led to my providing my readers with information on British India, why my grandfather was there and also on the reasons for sending the BEF to France.

Quite apart from any involvement in conflict, your relative may have had a long and interesting career, serving in many countries. If, for example, he was in the Navy, you might like to detail the ships he served on and the ports they visited; perhaps he had an association with a particularly well-known ship. Equally, your relative may have been in the Army and you could detail the history of his regiment or corps. My father as a young man worked for the Navy, Army and Air Force Institutes (NAAFI) in the early 1960s and also spent time aboard the Royal Yacht. This special association has provided me, as a family historian, with some engaging anecdotes and stories.

Campaign Medals
If your relatives have medals from campaigns they have been involved in, then you may wish to ask whether you could photograph them for inclusion in your story. You could then explain the origin of each and detail why your relative received it.

First World War medals of my great-grandfather Harry Cass.

HEARTH AND HOME

All our ancestors had a home, however humble, and with some research you should be able to describe what this was probably like. Luckily, due to a resurgence in interest in how we used to live it should be possible to learn about and comment on this aspect of an ancestor's life.

Television programme makers have bought the past to life with productions such as the series on the houses of 1900 and 1940 which show people living in those times and using period items. Even a television period dramas such as *Upstairs, Downstairs* and the recent film *Gosford Park* go some way in telling you and your readers of life in the times depicted. Indeed, these productions were highly praised for their attention to detail and use of consultants to ensure that period features were accurate.

Describing Your Ancestor's Home

If you are lucky enough to have an address to link your ancestor with, be it where he or she was born, whence was married or where died, you will be able to ascertain the sort of accommodation it was and comment on it by reference to local archives in your library or public record office. This is especially useful if the house or street no longer exists due to redevelopment. If this is the case, consider an enquiry to the local council or a newspaper office on the off chance that a photograph was taken before its demolition or a newspaper may have featured an article and published a photograph before it was pulled down.

Describe the home, whether the house was terraced or detached, flat-fronted or with a forecourt and whether it was two storeys or more. If the house is still there, take a photograph of it. Look on the outside and see whether there are any of the original features left, for example, a foot scraper or a chimney pot. Look for clues about what the house may have looked like to its inhabitants by examining other houses in the street for original features, such as a front door, sash windows or a tiled pathway or forecourt.

A friend of mine lives in a house where the original Victorian tiled forecourt, the tiled entrance hall floor as well as the original, black, iron fireplaces and tiled surrounds and hearths all remain. He answered a knock one day from an old lady who had lived there many years previously who asked if she could take a look at the house where she had spent so many years. She was amazed to find so many features that she remembered still intact.

By using reference books, especially those that claim to be source books for original fittings, you ought to be able to describe the interior. If you describe a small Victorian or Edwardian terraced house, for example, most probably the interior walls would have been painted a dark shade since any light coloured paint would have been difficult to keep clean, since the heating and cooking would almost certainly have been by coal fires. Depending on what period you are concerned with, there may have been plain, wooden floorboards or a linoleum covering. Wall-to-wall fitted carpets are quite modern, and, if they could be afforded, rugs would have been used. There would be no central heating, of course, but fires in a grate which would heat only one room, meaning that the rest of the house would have been cold.

Kitchens, or sculleries as they were sometimes called, were basic with maybe just a sink, a cupboard and a wooden table. Early housing would have no automatic supply of hot water, and all of it would have had to be boiled. Before the turn of the twentieth century most terraced housing would have had only an outside toilet and no bathroom at all. All baths would have had to be taken in a galvanized iron bath, most probably placed in front of the fire and filled with hot water from a bucket or a large pan from the stove. Three bedrooms would probably have been the maximum, with many having only two of equal size, both running off a tiny, square landing with their doors opposite to each other. One for the parents and the other for the children, probably divided by a sheet screen if the family consisted of boys and girls. Privacy was indeed a luxury in these homes.

Outside there may have been a courtyard, a backyard or a garden. If your ancestor had a garden he probably grew vegetables to supplement the family groceries. Many families kept chickens, ducks, rabbits or pigeons at the bottom of the garden for a home-grown supply of meat and eggs. They could also be used as a means of trade with the neighbours.

It is also worth bearing in mind that, for many of us, our ancestors were most likely not afforded the luxury of owning their homes; renting was much more the norm until the post-war Second World War period. I have rent books among family papers which, once translated from shillings and pence into decimal currency, are of interest in comparing rental prices then with those of today.

The middle classes enjoyed more comfort by far, and if your ancestor lived in the smart, large terraces or detached houses, he would have benefited from larger and airy rooms and probably also the services of a maid or two and a cook.

Following on from the current enthusiasm for the past and household antiques and items there should be plenty of source material on this subject for you to use.

Older Dwellings

If you can trace your ancestry back as far as the sixteenth, the seventeenth or the eighteenth century, it will be less likely that you will be able to find surviving examples of the type of housing your relatives lived in. Having said this, while poorer quality housing is likely not to have survived, our towns and cities still show some marvellous examples of Georgian, Jacobean and even Elizabethan housing. Villages may also have preserved many cottage dwellings. Two of my relatives currently live in a 400-year old cottage, and anyone tracing his or her history back to it would still be able to see original fireplaces and beams. I also remember on a trip to the village of Stedham, in West Sussex, coming across a tumbledown cottage and thinking what a wonderful discovery it would be to link one's own history to such a place. It will always be worth a visit to an area just in case the dwelling your ancestor lived in still survives. Should it not, if you can work out where it stood, this too would be worthy of comment for your readers. Even if you have no idea in what street they would have lived, you can still include a copy of an early street plan to show what the place was like at the time he lived there.

Using Wills as Sources

In trying to discover what possessions your ancestors may have had, do not neglect to examine wills as a source. You may think that all you can find out about an ancestor is a name scratched in a parish register, but if you can also locate a will you can bring him or her to life for your readers, as can be seen from the following example, they can be quite illuminating:

> I bequeath to John my one young cow and a ewe, an acre of rye and my best brass pot, and a wait and plough with all the gear that belong to it. Item I bequeath to Henry my son my next best pot and a chest. Item to Richard my son a brass pot, pair of sheets. Item I bequeath to John my said brother a platter, a candlestick, a scythe, a cob iron and a pair of tongs and a pair of bed stools ...

In 1591 John Ingolmells, of Great Carlton, was not only leaving his wife half his farm but he also provided well for his four daughters Isabell, Marie, Agnes and Elizabeth, which included 'one bed furnished to the value of 12 shillings and 4 pence' for each of the four.

On 4 February 1650 John Ingamells, also of Great Carlton and son of the above, bequeathed to his daughter Faith:

> ... twenty pounds, the white cow and the bed head in the house with the feather bed and a bolster, 3 pillows, 2 blankets, 2 coverlids, 2 sheets and curtains and valances, a great chest in the parlour with child bed linene and ten yards of linen of the 20 yards, 3 napkins wrought in blue, 4 pewter dubbers and the second brass pan and all her mother's clothes both wollen and linen ...

In 1692 Christopher Ingamells, of South Reston, left to his wife:

> half of my linen together with the bed in the far parlour and all that belongs to that bed and the bigger and better trunk in my house and the cupboard in the hall and half the pewter and the biggest brass pan and half a dozen chairs, three of one sort of and three of another and the lesser brass pot and the warming pan ...

Some even divided up the contents of their wardrobes; in 1565 Richard Ingolmells, of Saleby, left the following (presumably the recipients were his friends): 'Item to Johnne Robinson my best coette cote. Item I give to Walter Pinder my best fustian dublett. Item I give to Thomas Bailie my old russet cote that I wear. Item I give to Thomas Merykine my leather dublett.'

In 1646 William Ingamells, of Great Carlton, carried on the tradition: 'I bequeath to Richard Willson my brown briches and coat. To my brother (in law) Henry Clark my dublit briches and coat that I wear every day ...'

If your ancestors did not leave wills you should still be able to colour in your ancestors' lives by using reference books dealing with everyday domestic items in use at the time.

Inhabitants

Describing others who also lived in your ancestor's house is worth attempting and this can be done by using the census returns. Apart from those you might normally have expected to be there, there might also have been a lodger, a visiting relative or a friend of your ancestor. It has always amazed me how sometimes three generations of the same family lived in a two- or three-bedroom terraced house without any of today's modern domestic appliances.

It might also be worth a passing glance at who lived next door to your ancestors and a look down the street just in case they moved there to be near a brother or sister. On my father's side, two brothers married two sisters who lived next door to each other; with other siblings around it would have been difficult for the neighbours to find someone with whom to gossip about the family!

Relationships

Your ancestors' relationships are something that you may think are beyond your ability to comment upon with any authority, and to a degree, especially with regard to intimate relationships, you would be right. But there are relationships that your ancestors would have had that you will be able to make some broad assumptions about. Without actually having any material facts about long-dead relatives and simply by examining your family tree you should be able to comment on their type of life and the relations that existed between them. This is illustrated particularly well as regards married life and the ways in which your ancestors may have coped with their large families.

Married Life

With a lack of reliable means of birth control, families were generally larger in the past, but it is worth remembering that this was not necessarily by deliberate choice on the part of parents.

When I look back through my own family trees, I see families consisting of seven, eight, twelve or as many as fourteen children, with the mother often in childbirth almost continually from when she was sixteen until her forties. When considering families of this size, it is now difficult to image the sheer hard work needed in order to maintain them in the past, without today's domestic appliances and a house large enough to cope. If you have large families in your ancestry, even with some limited consideration of putting yourself in the shoes of either a mother or a sibling, it may be enlightening for future readers for you to comment on the difficulties that faced past generations of parents with large families.

Through my own delving I have been given some insight into what relationships between husbands and wives were like at the turn of the nineteenth century. A great-great cousin, Beatrice May Cass, born in 1896, remembered the following:

> Look at the size of the families they had then. Our mum's sister, next door but one, had twelve. And some woman round there, she had eighteen! They used to say, why did they have such big families? It was through ignorance. There weren't no pills on the go then. Wasn't much good the poor devils saying no, they weren't fussed about then like they are today. I don't think I saw my dad pick up a tea towel or wash up in my life. In fact, I don't remember our dad kissing our mum. Oh, he did when she came out of hospital when she'd had her operation. She was in the chair and he went over and kissed her and that's the first time I'd ever seen him kiss her. They were ignorant, they were, honestly.

On a more general point, wives and mothers in the past worked physically much harder than their counterparts today. You might like to comment on how demanding housework was. For instance, a whole day was given over to washing; 'wash day' invariably meant the women of the household slaving over coppers of boiling water, scrubbing boards and feeding clothing through mangles – think back to a life without the bliss of washing machines, electric dryers, electric irons and vacuum cleaners.

Parents and Children

The relationship between parents and their children has changed dramatically over the centuries. For the poor, since the lack of adequate means of birth control meant that children came along with regular monotony, parents sent them out to work as soon as they were old enough to help to support the whole family unit with the few pence they could earn. This was done out of necessity – my great-grandfather is shown in the 1891 census, aged 13, as a 'coal miner', and, according to his son, his father had told him he had started in the mines when he was aged only 11. Needless to say, this is in stark contrast with today, with parents often supporting their children through school and university, some of these not starting full-time employment until they are well into their 20s.

Child mortality was much higher in the past than it generally is now – a great-great grandmother had four babies die, each within a year of its birth from one contagious ailment or another. Nevertheless, a common theme seems to emerge within families; all were poor but there was still a sense that, despite this, there were still certain standards to be kept, children were fed as well as was feasible, they were brought up to be clean and taught to be mannerly:

> [Step-father] George Palmer never drunk and he never swore. Never used bad language. And yet he used to get with some of the roughest people that used to stand over Charlotte Street and Paradise Street. He used to go with the roughest

people there was, and yet he never used to use bad language at home. That's why our mum wouldn't let us use bad language ... He always cleaned the grate, you could see your face in the fireplace and he'd clean his boots just to stand down the garden to watch his pigeons ...

From those I have interviewed, I have observed children alluding to adults inhabiting a 'secret world', where certain things would not be spoken of in a child's hearing and some subjects (especially those of a sexual nature) were strictly taboo:

Kids, when they're trying to find out about sex and that, I always thought that they cut you open, lifted the baby out and sewed it back and that was that. Well, there was about four of us discussing all this, so I said, 'I'll tell you what, our Lucy's just had a baby, I'll go in and ask her, she'll tell me and I'll let you know.' So I went in and I said, 'Lucy, well, you know you've just had a baby – yes – well, tell me, how do they come out, how are they born?' She said, 'Well, they comes out the same way as they goes in!' And I was none the wiser. I wasn't any wiser because I didn't know what happened to get a baby! I never knew a thing.

In those days you couldn't ask your mother any questions because, if you did, you didn't get any answers. You daren't stand by mum if she was talking to anybody. If you went indoors and mum was talking to a neighbour you had to turn round and walk out. You used to have to say, 'Excuse me.' And if mum was talking at the front door to a neighbour and you stood there, she'd say, 'And what do you want?', 'Nothing mum.' 'Off!' She wouldn't let you listen to a conversation at all. There was nothing discussed, not like today, everything is discussed in the family, nothing at all was ever discussed with mum.

Despite their poverty, such families still strived to maintain their own high moral standards in ways that now seem harsh:

They would stone you in them days, if you were having a baby and weren't married. Poor girl down our street, her mother was ever so posh, and that poor girl got in the family way, and her name stank! Nowadays, they don't take any notice, do they? She was ever such a nice girl. But you'd have thought it was the end of the world, but not now. My goodness, that was years ago. But talk about when that poor girl had to get married! When girls got in the family way they were the worst of the worst. The poor girls couldn't hold their heads up, but now, it's a recognized thing.

A funny thing with our mum – I don't think she ever wanted any of us to get married. If she'd had her way, she would have had us all in the house living together, and that would have been her ideal way of life, to have a big house and have all the family round her. I can't ever remember her really wanting us to marry anyone. I don't know why. It's only looking back that I can see it. I don't know whether she was so possessive with us because she worked so hard to bring us up, because she did work hard, none worked harder.

The next statement was probably true of a lot of large working-class families, with mothers so busy with the daily grind that they had no time to spare even for affection: 'And yet I can't ever remember our mum, when we were children, she never ill-treated us or anything, but I can never remember her showing us a lot of affection. Probably she didn't have time for it, with all the kids.'

It may also be worth noting how relationships between parents and children have changed over the years. There was formerly often a prevailing sense that 'children should be seen and not heard', and I can certainly remember this being said to me on a few occasions. If you can use oral history, compare you relatives' relations with their parents with those that you have with your own; take this, for example:

> My father was very strict. Until I started working, every Sunday I had to get up and go to church, first thing in the morning on Sunday. And in the afternoon and in the evening. Three times on a Sunday. All the family, all except mother, who had to stay behind and cook the dinner.

Relationships between Siblings

You may also wish to observe the fact that in some large families there was often many years between the eldest child and the youngest. For example, my grandmother, who was born in 1908, was aged 24 when her youngest brother was born in 1932. By this time she had married and had just had her own daughter; so her brother had a niece who was of the same age as he.

The eldest children in the household were generally looked upon to help with child care and to take on the responsibility for the rest of the children in order to free the parents to earn a living. This could mean that girls as young as 10 or 11 were obliged to look after their families, including babies and young children, for many years into their late teens. This was all very well if you were suited for it, but, according to my great-aunt, my grandmother obviously resented being used in this way and even went into service as a means of escape:

> Lucy went into service. When mum was going to have Ray, I think it was, she said she wasn't going to stop home and look after any more children and she went into service over the Isle of Wight ... I think once Lucy left school she didn't want to know, she didn't want to have to be bothered with the family and she went into service.

HEALTH

You may wonder what relevance the health of your ancestors would have for your readers, but how many of us have been asked at some point by a doctor, 'Does anyone else in the family suffer from this?' And advances in medicine

74

already hint at the prospect of delving into the genes of your immediate ancestors to tell you whether or not you may be susceptible to a particular inheritable condition or illness.

Before you think that the health of your ancestors is a subject that you can afford to ignore, if for no other reason than that it is something you that feel you cannot comment on, their health could be closely related to their social or working environment, which, if you are short of material, could give you something more to probe. You may think that the health of your ancestors much depended on their wealth, but as is illustrated by the death of Albert, the Prince Consort in 1861, from typhoid, such illnesses struck both the low- and the high-born and wealth was no protector. Such illnesses were largely the result of current living and working conditions.

The remarks by a great-uncle of mine born in 1909 are interesting and could be relevant to many families in the early 1900s:

> Child mortality was high then because they didn't know what was wrong with them. Often the doctors knew what was wrong but couldn't do anything about it. I had appendicitis and I wasn't expected to live, but now it's nothing. There was tuberculosis. People couldn't afford to convalesce and they died. People used to die with measles. Mayda had diphtheria and she wasn't expected to live.

When I study the death certificates of my ancestors, among the expected and usual causes of death of the elderly, are two which provided me with useful material and made it possible for me to expand on their deaths for my readers. One was of my great-great grandmother who died in 1902 in the imbecile ward of the Portsmouth Union Workhouse.

While this fact surprised me at the time, it was nevertheless something I could not ignore and I wanted to find out more about how she died and, most importantly, how she came to be there. Unfortunately, this was one area where my search came to a halt. Although I was given permission by the local authority to have searches made of the records of the workhouse while the 100-year rule was still in force, the documents themselves had not survived. There was simply no more personal information that I could give my readers about the life of Isabella Ingamells. In the light of this, I decided that the only thing I could do to tell her story was to introduce a short 'essay' on the history and conditions of the workhouse system in which she ended her days.

As to what might have caused her to be incarcerated in the grimly named imbecile ward is a matter for speculation. She had been a mother of six children, with only two surviving. Her cause of death was stated as 'mania exhaustion', which, at best, suggests some kind of depression and, at worst, some kind of mental or nervous breakdown, enough to have caused her death. This term is particularly unhelpful since promiscuous women, epileptics and the weak-witted could have also found themselves in such wards.

At the turn of the last century the understanding of mental frailty was still limited, with only primitive, if any, treatment being given to patients. There was little or no acknowledgement of the different types of mental illness nor of the degree of severity, thus allowing for the depressed and the eccentric to be held along with violent and dangerous lunatics, all living together and, despite their several conditions, all considered as deserving the tag of imbecile or lunatic. The most worrying thing about my ancestor's being in this place was that she may have been admitted following some form of anxiety or depression which was only exacerbated by her being so confined. Following from my research, I concluded that, if you were not mad when you went in, the chances are that it would not be long before you were. Regrettably it is probably the case that, although unfortunate for an ancestor of yours so treated, the more out of the ordinary his or her death was, the more material you are likely to have to convey to your readers.

Wealth

The wealth of your ancestors may have varied considerably over the generations. While two separate branches of my own family survived real poverty (especially by today's standards), another was apparently wealthy in the seventeenth and the eighteenth century.

Unfortunately for our ancestors, on death, their possessions, money, houses and land were often divided equally among the children, and, if the family was large or a second marriage was involved, to receive only a fifth or a sixth share (often less in much larger families) of an estate could soon reduce the wealth of one branch of a family.

Certainly, because your family displays no sign of family wealth now does not imply that in the past they were not doing well. Indeed, the fact that you are here today shows that, money or no money, your own line of the family has shown the ability to survive.

Crime and Punishment

If an ancestor was poor, hungry and cold he may well have taken a chance to make his lot a little better, and, with poaching and the stealing of wood from forests being among the most common 'crimes', he may well have fallen foul of the law. Perhaps unfortunately for your ancestor, in eighteenth-century Britain a large number of these, to us, petty crimes were punishable by death. Although such sentences were passed, a high percentage of death sentences were reduced by reprieve or pardon to transportation. Equally of interest, you may be able to establish that an ancestor was a victim of crime. In either case, if your ancestors had contact with the law in the past you could use the following pointers to help in describing their probable experience.

Before the existence of police forces it was left to each parish to employ constables to investigate reported crimes and to report these to the magistrates. Once arrested, unless the suspect could produce an assurance to appear in court, he would remain in goal until the court sat.

If you suspect or know that an ancestor had been in prison, the records in county record offices can be searched. The National Archives at Kew will have some records, mainly from the state institutions such as Parkhurst, Pentonville and Dartmoor. Accounts of prisons, prison hulks, prison life and criminal records research can be found in family history magazine articles and from websites, most notably the John Howard site.

Courts
The less serious crimes were tried at quarter sessions courts held in county, borough and city jurisdictions up to four times a year: at Epiphany (January), Easter (March/April), summer (July) and Michaelmas (October). More serious crimes, including capital crimes, were tried at assize courts in spring (March) and summer (July/August). In London, the Old Bailey Sessions were held more frequently. If an ancestor was unlucky enough to have been convicted of a crime you may wish to include details of the court process in your story.

Punishments
There were three main punishments for serious crimes: hanging, imprisonment (on land or in a hulk) and transportation; lesser punishments were: whipping, being confined to the stocks and being ducked in a 'stool'.

Hanging
The act of theft could carry a hefty price for anyone convicted in the eighteenth and the early nineteenth century, with crimes such as poaching and sheep- or horse-stealing carrying the death penalty. Gibbets were dotted in the countryside and in townships alike and may show on old maps; some of the sites such as that of Coombe on the Wiltshire–Berkshire border, even exist today.

Punishment by hanging saw the criminal being driven to his death in a horse-drawn cart. His hands were tied behind his back and, at the place of execution, the rope was placed around his neck. A hood was placed over his head and, on a signal, the horses were whipped up and the cart sped off, the violent jolting of the rope as his footing was lost left him swinging from the rope. Bodies were left to hang for an hour before being cut down and, in the case of murderers, sold for medical research. This punishment was carried out in public until the mid- to the late nineteenth century, after which it took place within the confines of a prison.

Imprisonment
In the eighteenth century many British gaols were managed by private individuals, employing gaolers who made their living by charging prisoners for rooms, food and any other comforts they could afford to buy from the gaoler. The conditions in many gaols were filthy, with overcrowding and poorly-ventilated rooms which would hold both men and women. Prisoners were often kept close to starvation on a diet of bread and water, often wearing ragged

clothing with little or no bedding. Some would have been chained to the floor or wall.

The prison reformer John Howard undertook to visit almost every prison in England between 1770 and 1790 to investigate their state. He wrote this description of the conditions he found:

> Convicts are generally stout, robust young men, who have been accustomed to free diet, tolerable lodgings and vigorous exercise. These are ironed, and thrust into close offensive dungeons, and there chained down, some of them without straw or other bedding; in which they continue, in winter, sixteen or seventeen hours out of the twenty-four, in utter inactivity, and immersed in the noxious effluvia of their own bodies ...Their diet is at the same time low and scanty; they are generally without firing; and the powers of life soon become incapable of resisting so many caused of sickness and despair ... Their destruction is not only unjust; it is inconsistent with prudence and sound policy. They might, no doubt, be useful at home or abroad, if proper care were taken of them in prison, to keep them healthy and fit for labour. But certain it is that many of those who survive their long confinement, are by it rendered incapable of working. Some of them by scourbutic [sic] distempers, others by their toes mortified, or quite rotted from their feet, many instances of which I have seen.

Under growing pressure from prison reformers such as Howard, some improvements were introduced during the late 1700s. Despite an improvement in the conditions and diet, it was reported in the Wiltshire Statistics of Crime in 1850 that, since 1835, prisoners had endured the following conditions:

> The prisoners now, except when at labour, are confined in their cells, nor do they associate but when they are about to proceed to chapel, or are exercising in the yard. In this latter case, they walk the yard about two hours morning and afternoon; six only allowed to take exercise at the same period, and then at a distance of 12 or 15 yards from each other. Silence is strictly enjoined and punishments, by stopping of food, or close confinement or whipping, awarded for any infringement of the rules.

Transportation

The system of transporting convicts from Britain derived from a 1597/98 Act of Parliament which provided for 'rogues to be banished out of this realm ... and conveyed unto such parts beyond the seas as shall be at any time hereafter assyned for that purpose.'

From the establishment of Virginia in 1607, small numbers of convicts were sent there and to the other American colonies. An Act of 1717 allowed convicts to choose exile instead of branding, whipping or execution. Until the start of the American War of Independence in 1775, prisoners who chose transportation, in later years as many as a thousand annually, were taken there. From that date on a new strategy decreed that prisoners either went on hulks or were sent to Africa, Tasmania or New South Wales in Australia. Between 1719 and 1772 it is estimated that 30,000 convicts were transported from England (source: Michael Flynn, *The Second Fleet*). The final shipment of 800 arrived at Swan River in Western Australia in 1867, the last of the 150,000 to be transported from England. If they survived the journey and their punishment, many of those deported went on to lead a new life (see the Appendix for websites containing information on the biographies of transportees).

As a temporary solution to the problem of overcrowding in England's gaols, legislation was passed in 1776 which provided for dismantled ships (hulks) to be used as temporary places of detention. Men held were held on them to serve their sentence or await transportation.

Sourcing Material on Criminal Ancestors

Fascinating sources for ancestors who committed crimes include the county statistics of crime, prison registers and the sentences handed down. These and other, related documents can be found at your local record office.

As an example of what can be discovered, the following is an extract from the Wiltshire Statistics of Crime from 1801 to 1850:

1806 Hilary Sessions
John Aust was indicted under the Act of 6 Geo. III for cropping and spoiling timber trees in the night time, which makes the offence felony, and empowers the court to transport for seven years. The prosecutor, however, in this case, begged a lenient sentence, as he wished merely to undeceive the lower order of people, who fancied that for such offences only a small fine could be inflicted. The court listened to the appeal and sentenced him to six months.

What makes these documents so fascinating is the amount of detail they may contain, including details of the victim and comments on the perpetrator's demise:

1810 Summer Assizes
Execution of Thomas Jones (alias Hughes) and Richard Francis for Burglary

These prisoners broke into the shop of Mr Bennett, a jeweller and silversmith at Salisbury, and stole there from a large quantity of gold and silver watches, chains, seals and articles of jewellery. Their apprehension was effected in the following manner: As the coach from Taunton to London was proceeding near Sutton Scotney, Jones and Francis came from under a hedge with a bundle in their hands, and hailing the coachman, engaged to go to London with him as outside passengers. The guard, who had heard of the robbery in his journey through Salisbury, immediately suspected them, and mentioned his suspicions to an inside passenger; in consequence of which, when the coach arrived at Egham, they were given into the custody of a constable, and by him conveyed to Bow Street, London, where the prosecutor, who had arrived beforehand, identified the contents of the bundles as his property. It subsequently transpired that Jones was an escaped convict. The conduct of Francis from his condemnation to his execution was very exemplary and devout, but that of Jones was very indifferent, even to the last moment. When, at the foot of the ladder, he was greeted with a wish that he might obtain forgiveness of his Maker, he replied coolly, 'Thank you' in about the same manner as he would have done to a common salutation, and when the rope was around his neck, he looked coolly round and threw his hat among the people. Owing to some displacement of the rope, and his light weight, Jones died with much protracted suffering.

These records may also contain much detail concerning the crimes committed:

1836 Lent Assizes
Execution of Henry Wynn, for Murder

Wynn was a mean-looking little man, with a vulgar unintellectual countenance, and obtained his living by travelling the country with various articles, accompanied by Eliza Jones, his victim. On the day of the murder she had left him on the road and gone towards Highworth, in company with a blind man, and another woman. On Wynn's arriving at Highworth, he found Eliza Jones sitting on a bench, between the woman and the blind man, and being rendered jealous on this account, he took out a clasp knife and deliberately stabbed her in the side, from the effects of which, in some hours, she died. In his defence he said, 'He did not know what urged him to do it, or how he did it; he took the knife out of his pocket, but how he struck at her he did not know, his reason was gone.' He became penitent while in prison and confessed, that throughout his life he had been so hardened a sinner, that he feared the Almighty would never listen to his prayers for forgiveness. He walked to the scaffold with much firmness, united in the last prayers with that kind of composure in which he would perform any common act of duty, and coolly requested the executioner to remove his cravat. The executioner having done so, placed it in Wynn's bosom, when he said that such a proceeding was useless, as he should want it no more. Then firmly mounting the scaffold, requested that every thing might be expeditiously managed, threw the cravat out of his bosom among the crowd, and having ejaculated a few words, ceased to exist. His body was interred within the wall of Fisherton gaol, in the first-class misdemeanants' yard, in accordance with the act of parliament, which legalised dissection, and annulled the dissection and mutilation of the body of murderers. This is the first body so disposed of.

The next example deals with the less common practice of wife selling:

1833 Michaelmas Sessions
This case relates to a man named Isaac Spencer, who, believing that selling his wife publicly in the market place, with a halter around her neck, would have the full force of a divorce legally obtained, took his wife (equally willing to try a

change of circumstances) into the public market at Melksham, and there disposed of her for 2s. 6d. [25p] to a man named William Watts. Both were committed to prison for the offence, but Watts was acquitted.

Spencer received three months' imprisonment and was fined 20 shillings (£1.00).

Should an ancestor have fallen foul of the law or was a victim of crime, the chances are that it was recorded.

MIGRATION

In investigating my own family history, I had gone back only three generations to find, on the 1881 census return, that my great-great grandfather was born, not in Portsmouth where I lived, but in Shaftesbury. At the time, this rather upset my idea that the family had probably been long established in Portsmouth, and it was also inconvenient to have to travel to another county to carry out further research. When I eventually visited Shaftesbury it became difficult for me to imagine why anyone would have wanted to leave there and its beautiful countryside to move to the Rudmore area of Portsmouth, which, at the time they would have migrated there, was full of tightly packed, terraced cottages that ran down to the industrialized quayside. Research on the socio-economic conditions that prevailed in the 1870s in rural England gave me the answer to my question.

James Cass lived in Shaftesbury and worked as an agricultural labourer in 1871, as had his father before him and his mother before then. His father, it seems, had been forced to turn his hand to anything – perhaps to prevent the family from having to go to the workhouse, the Alchester. Several documentary sources showed that he was, variously, a labourer, rag dealer, pedlar, hawker and, lastly, by the time of his death aged 78, a stone mason's labourer. His son James must have begun to struggle to bring up his growing family against a backdrop of pauperdom in rural Dorset, living in a small, two-up, two-down, stone, tied cottage, with no running water, in St. James Street.

In the 1870s there was a run of bad harvests, and these, along with the farming of the American prairies, new faster and cheaper shipping from the USA and the development overseas of wool growing, led to a depression in English agriculture. The country also received a flood of labourers from Ireland, with the result that wages dropped severely for farm labourers. Because of the lack of work opportunities, bad harvests and a reduced demand for British produce, there was a general decline of whole countryside and village communities. Agricultural labourers were made redundant and evicted from their tied cottages. Between 1861 and 1901 there was a marked decrease in the number of rural male labourers in England and Wales. It would have been conditions such as these that forced James Cass and his family to move to Portsmouth to seek work on the coal barges, exchanging the green fields and rolling hills of Dorset, for Portsmouth and the grey-blue sea of the Solent.

On another side of my family, the same conditions lured my great-great grandparents away from the village of Evercreech, which lies among some of the most beautiful countryside in Somerset. George Green left the life of the agricultural labourer to find work either as a coal miner or on the railway at Mountain Ash in Wales, a small village whose population grew in size from 1,614 in 1841 to 11,463 by 1871 due to the incoming labour force.

The great migration of labour had a huge impact on country life. The small communities that made up the villages were drastically thinned out as the young and fit moved away. This left no one to pass on the customs, rituals, songs and folklore that had been handed down from generation to generation, affecting village and country life for ever. Sadly, as in the case of Evercreech, by the turn of the nineteenth century there were few inhabitants left who could claim to have any long-established, local family connexions remaining as the newcomers arrived.

If an ancestor migrated from one part of the country to another, consider what method of transport would have been used by him or her and comment on this. Before the age of steam, your ancestor would certainly have moved any long distance by cart or stage coach. Look on old maps to find the routes these coaches would have taken and you may be able to chart your ancestor's own route.

EMIGRATION

You may discover that your ancestors emigrated and, if they did, search for a reason why they may done so. They may have emigrated for economical or political reasons. For example, a large number of Huguenots moved from France in the mid seventeenth century to escape persecution for their religious beliefs. If you discover that you have Huguenot ancestry you should visit the Huguenot Library at University College London for further genealogical material.

In the mid-1800s a large population of Irishmen and women emigrated from Ireland to America and England to escape poverty and starvation. These are but two instances of large population movements that may affect your research.

Many British people emigrated to the new worlds of the USA, Australia and New Zealand, seemingly undaunted by the long sea journeys involved and uncertainty about what they would find when they arrived. If your ancestors emigrated try to discover how they travelled, when, and where they arrived and settled.

Enforced Emigration: Transportation
This has been mentioned above and it may be that some ancestors emigrated forcibly through transportation or were one of the ships that carried convicts to Australia, Tasmania and the USA. Much work has been done in tracing those who were on board these 'convict ships' and one illustration of this is

Michael Flynn's book *The Second Fleet – Britain's Grim Convict Armada of 1790*, which gives many detailed biographies of the crews and convicts on these ships.

SLAVERY

If your ancestors came long ago from West Africa, then their enforced emigration into slavery in Europe, the West Indies or America will be of enormous interest to you.

Hundreds of thousands of men, women and children were brutally kidnapped, beaten and transported to endure many years if not a lifetime of slavery. This human trafficking started in the 1560s and carried on into the 1800s. Vast profits were made from slavery and some families based their wealth on the backs of the enslaved, and English cities such as Bristol and Liverpool grew prosperous because of this trade in human cargo.

Fortunately for the family historian, some slaves wrote their autobiography and these are generally available and valuable sources for contemporary accounts. One such is from Olaudah Equiano (also known as Gustavus Vassa) who was kidnapped by raiders from West Africa in 1755 aged 10. Olaudah was taken to the West Indies but eventually sold to a British naval officer who took him to Nova Scotia and then to England. His master renamed him Gustavus Vassa, after the Swedish king. Olaudah was finally sold to a Quaker, Robert King, by whom he was eventually freed. Olaudah survived his terrible experiences as a slave, learned English and wrote his autobiography, which was published in 1789.

USING ESSAYS

In order to help you in telling the story of your family, you may wish to punctuate your history with essays. Do not be put off by the word 'essay' – think of it as the bringing together of various pieces of information to give your readers an understanding of a particular subject. For example, if you know that a relative was involved in the Battle of Waterloo, you may wish to write a chapter or part of one called 'The Battle of Waterloo' and write about it, its cause and its outcome. You could use this to introduce readers to this time in the life of your ancestor, and, even if you do not know what part they played in the battle, by writing about it in the way suggested you leave readers to use their own imagination, having set the scene. You can then continue to tell the life of your ancestor and carry on from the essay. You could do this at a number of stages in the lives of your ancestors and thus smooth the transition from one period or generation to another. But even if your ancestors lived a more quiet life, you can still use this technique to convey information about their lives.

Anyone who traces their family history through the nineteenth and into the twentieth century will be able to expand on the British Empire, when Britain ruled a quarter of the world including the India subcontinent, large parts of

Asia, Africa and Australasia. This seems almost incomprehensible today, and so it would not be inappropriate to inform or remind your readers of this, a marked contrast to England today when many of us think of ourselves as islanders. The British Empire, with the monarch ruling as Emperor or Empress of India, existed only a century ago.

Another relevant topic is the rigid class system that prevailed throughout the nineteenth and the twentieth century Britain, now much reduced in significance. Whatever background your ancestors came from, there is plenty of material from which to draw a picture of what life was like, for example, at the end of the nineteenth century. If your relatives were lucky enough to be in the upper classes, their lives would have been dictated by strict social protocols. How they should address servants – if at all, and what they should wear at any given time of day. That famous authority Mrs Beeton, as well as advice on cookery, gave the mistress of the house instructions on how to leave the dinner table and other aspects of etiquette. If your ancestors were of the middle class there were still more protocols to be observed, since these were obsessed with 'respectability'; but if they lower in the social order, they too were probably aware of the importance of 'knowing their place', but also with making sure that their neighbours did not get above themselves. These were the times when a gentleman could be recognized by the clothes he wore, and the middle classes were largely determined by their professions – the superior occupations were those of city 'gent', doctor, lawyer, minister of religion, along with the commissioned ranks in the Army or the Navy. The poor, in stark contrast, put their children out to work to help to feed the family, and, in the most dire cases, sold them.

In writing your family's story the subject of class should not be ignored; what follows came from my great aunt, who was aged 14 in 1920: 'I went to the Air Balloon pub when I was 14 years old. I slept in, that was the worst part of it, if you slept in, you didn't get much time to yourself. That's all there was, service or go in the factory. I didn't want to go in the factory.' The choice between 'service' and factory employment as the only options available to young girls seems to have been fairly typical for the lower classes.

One event that threw men of all classes together was the First World War. You only have to look around the country today, from Eton College to the memorial on the village green, there are shocking numbers of names of the rich and the poor who died alongside each other. If you can only go back three or four generations you will find a relative or two who served in one service or another during the war. Some would say that this was the beginning of the end for the upper and the middle classes and their styles of life.

The First World War also brought women to the fore: if they were not nursing the wounded, they were in the munitions factories, employed in clerical work or as typists, or as bus conductresses. Women were earning more and thereby their families benefited from being fed better. Women's contribution in the First World War stood them in good stead as they fought too for universal suffrage.

To ease the transition in your history from one century to another or from one ancestor to another, you could insert a brief essay to outline the important events at the time at which you want to leave one ancestor to pick up the life of the next. The examples above should help you in this.

THE USE OF LITERATURE AND POETRY

Dickens, Hardy, Austen, George Eliot, the Brontës, Defoe, Wells and Fielding, to name but a few, all wrote novels describing the everyday lives of their characters in their contemporary surroundings, making them particularly useful as social commentators. Novelists can provide you with passages you can use to illustrate and enrich the story of your family, especially when an ancestor shared a particular situation or occupation with a character in a novel. These extracts can be used to give a flavour of times long past and a window on the world as seen by the novelist themselves.

Supposing, for example, you wished to describe the last visitation of the plague in England in 1665. As well as other accounts, you could use extracts from Daniel Defoe's book *A Journal of the Plague Year*, which, although written as though Defoe was an eyewitness to events in London in 1665, was actually written in 1722. Defoe was in fact only 4 years old at the time of the plague that he writes so hauntingly and knowledgeably about. Despite the fact it is a novel, the book could have a basis in fact. Defoe's uncle, a saddler named Henry Foe, lived at Aldgate in east London at the time of the plague, and it is as a saddler that Defoe recounts his story, which suggests that Foe recounted to his nephew the terrible scenes he witnessed:

> At another house ... in the street next within Aldgate, a whole family was shut up and locked in, because the maid servant was taken sick; the Master of the House had complained by his Friends to the next Alderman and to the Lord Mayor, and had consented to have the maid carried to the Pest House but was refused, so the door was marked with a red cross, a padlock on the outside, and a Watchman set to keep the door according to public order.

Defoe enhanced his credentials as a social commentator by embarking on a tour of England during which he journeyed from London to Lands End, through the south-eastern counties and East Anglia, as well as Yorkshire and the north-west, writing about the places and things he witnessed.

Social commentators such as William Cobbett, who journeyed around the country largely in the footsteps of Defoe, and the diarist Samuel Pepys may also provide you with contemporary eyewitness accounts, if you can trace ancestors back to the times when they wrote. If, for example, an ancestor lived in London in September 1666, Pepys would give you an account of the Great Fire:

> I after supper walked in the dark down to Tower Street and there saw it all on fire, at the Trinity House on that side, and the Dolphin Tavern on this side, which was

very near us; and the fire with extraordinary vehemence. Now begins the practice of blowing up of houses in Tower Street, those next to the Tower which at first did frighten people more than anything; but it stopped the fire where it was done, it bringing down the houses in the same places they stood ...

While such sources as Cobbett and Pepys are more properly writers of social and local history, if you are able to illustrate your story with material from contemporary sources it will lend authenticity to the period you are endeavouring to describe. Social historians too, are good sources of social history. In 1851 Henry Mayhew, journalist and social historian, wrote a series of articles for the *Morning Chronicle* entitled 'The Great World of London'. Formerly an editor of Punch, Mayhew walked the streets of London talking to the working-class people about their lives, aspirations and dreams and noted what they had to say. Mayhew spoke to weavers, chimney sweeps, prostitutes, beggars and thieves and recorded them in their own words. For anyone with roots in London, *Mayhew's London* and *London's Underworld* are essential reading since Mayhew takes the reader street by street, through lanes and alleyways to meet the poor.

The use of the word 'poetry' in the title of this section may appear strange and you may wonder how you might use it in your family story – and even why you should; but it may, nevertheless, have a place. Poetry has the ability to communicate thoughts and feelings in a subtle but succinct way; it can provide an understanding of a particular subject in such a way as to express precisely the tone or mood you yourself would wish to convey. Many poets wrote poems about places, people, occupations and situations that could be relevant to your ancestors. For example, the nineteenth-century poet Thomas Hood wrote in *The Lay of the Labourer* of the determination of the labourer to do any task set him in order to avoid living off the parish and going to the workhouse:

> No parish money, or loaf,
> No pauper badges for me,
> A son of the soil, by right of toil
> Entitled to my fee.
> No alms I ask, give me my task:
> Here are the arm, the leg,
> The strength, the sinews of a Man,
> To work, and not to beg.

If you are in any doubt as to the use of poetry in your story, you may wish to consider using the poignant and moving work of the poets of the two World Wars if any of your ancestors were involved in them.

5 Ideas for Constructing and Writing Your Family History

Making a Start

Using the suggestions contained in the previous chapters of this book, you should now be casting a critical eye over all the material and data you have amassed in order to extract from it the story of your family. It is now time to decide where your story will start – either from yourself working backward or from your most distant ancestor and work forward.

To help you to plan your story, it may be useful to use a 'timeline' to map out your history. Let us assume that you can trace your family history back to the 1800s and you have decided to introduce the story from the first relative of whom you know, who was born in 1814. Write 1814 at the top of the line, the name of your ancestor and the fact that this was his or her baptism date. You can then repeat this for the date of marriage, the birth of children and death. Some general local and social history research will then enable you to fill in the gaps between these dates with details of events that you know happened in their lives and events that occurred either nationally or internationally and that would have affected their lives.

You should now have a framework upon which to write your story.

Beginning with the Facts

In order to overcome the initial barrier of what to write or how to write it, it may be a useful to begin by just writing down all the factual material you have on one ancestor, for example, extracting information contained in birth, marriage and death certificates:

> Thomas Henry Ingamells was born on the 8th July 1855 at Hundleby Fen Allotment, West Fen, near Boston, Lincolnshire. He was the son of Henry and Ann Ingamells and was their second child.

1800	Washington becomes US President
1805	Steam locomotive developed
1805	Battle of Trafalgar
1812	Napoleon retreats from Russia
1814	**Charles Cass born in Shaftesbury, Dorset**
1819	Peterloo Massacre
1821	Famine in Ireland
1828	Wellington becomes Prime Minister
1829	William IV ascends the throne
1831	Cholera epidemic
1834	Tolpuddle Martyrs arrested
1836	**Charles Cass married Caroline Tanswell**
1837	Queen Victoria ascends the throne
1838	**Sarah Cass born**
1839	**Thirza Cass born**
1846	Corn Laws repealed
1848	**James Cass born**
1851	Great Exhibition
1853	Start of Crimean War
1861	Start of American Civil War
1867	**James married Martha Mitchell**
1868	Gladstone becomes Prime Minister
1873	**James and Martha move to Portsmouth**
1874	Disraeli become Prime Minister
1879	Zulu War
1887	**Caroline Cass died**
1887	Queen Victoria's Golden Jubilee
1894	**Charles Cass died**

Timeline for the Cass family.

On the 8th January 1884 Thomas Henry Ingamells's son Herbert was born. The mother called herself Isabella Ingamells and they lived at 11 Britannia Street, Leeds. Thomas Henry was described as a cartman.

On the 25th August 1890 Thomas Henry Ingamells married Isabella Sims, a widow. They married at Portsmouth Registry Office and were both aged 35 years. They lived at 13 Blenheim Street, Southsea. Thomas's occupation was a carman and his father Henry Ingamells was described as a farm bailiff. The bride's father was Charles White, a mariner.

On the 14th September 1890 a daughter, Ada Florence was born to Thomas Henry and Isabella Ingamells. They resided at 13 Blenheim Street, Southsea.

On the 13th July 1902 Isabella Ingamells died of 'mania exhaustion' in the Imbecile Ward of the Portsmouth Workhouse Infirmary. She was 47 years old.

Thomas Ingamells was present at the time of her death and was residing at 50 Waldron Road.

On 6th November 1910, Thomas Henry married his second wife, Elizabeth Fanny Allen, a spinster aged 33. They were married at Portsea Parish Church and Elizabeth Jane Ingamells and Benjamin Charles Ingamells were witnesses. Thomas Henry was described as a carman.

On the 5th December 1928 Thomas Henry Ingamells died at 71 Clarence Street, Portsmouth. He died from bronchitis. His wife, Elizabeth was present at the time of his death.

If you know when a relative was born, when he or she married and died, you have your beginning, middle and end for this particular person which will help you to construct his or her life story. By so using the factual material you will see where you can fill in the gaps between these significant events. You have now begun to write your family history.

You now need to build on your facts. Using your timeline, start by examining the dates and expand upon when your ancestor was born and what was then happening the world. Use the suggestions in this book to make your story interesting instead of presenting merely a series of names and dates and bring your ancestors to life for your readers.

INTRODUCING YOUR STORY

You have planned your story and begun to write. Do remember that, although your ancestors need to appear in chronological order, you do not necessarily have to write about them in the same way. Once you have written out your timeline as a guide, you can move between times and ancestors as you acquire the necessary information to build up your story.

Once you start to write about the lives of your relatives you will need to consider how to set out the first paragraphs that will introduce your readers to the story. If you need some help in this you may wish to consider some of the following examples as a way to get you started:

Your first paragraph could begin: 'The charting of this family's history starts in 1814 among the rolling Dorset countryside, in the town of Shaftesbury. Charles Cass was baptized in St. Peter's Church, in the parish of St. James, Shaftesbury in 1814 ...' This will introduce your readers immediately to the place in history where your story will unfold and take them to the present time.

Alternatively, you may wish to start in this way: 'Ancestors sharing our family name appear in the county of Lincolnshire as far back as 1234, with the first official recording naming Peter de Ingoldmells and his wife Alice, who were mentioned in the Final Concords of Henry III ...' Or 'I was born on the 4th July 1964, the great-great-great-great granddaughter of Ann Cass, our earliest known ancestor ...'

Simple research may tell you on what day of the week your ancestor was born and even what the weather was like, and so you may wish to start like this: 'On a sunny day on Monday, the 11th June 1644, Ebeneezer Jones was born in Cardiff to Sarah and William Jones ...' Or, more dramatically 'On the 31st August 1908, a violent storm broke out across the whole of southern England, causing great chaos and destruction. At number 12 Clarence Street, Portsmouth, lived Ada Florence Ingamells, heavily pregnant with her first child Lucy, who was born ...'

Any of these styles could be used, substituting the details of your own family. You can begin your story as calmly or dramatically as you like. Draw on local, national and international events to set the scene and give your readers little details that they would not otherwise either know or associate with the time of your ancestors. I begin one of my own family history's in the following way:

> The family name of Ingamells originates and is unique to the county of Lincolnshire. Along the Lincolnshire coast is the village of Ingoldmells, from which the name Ingamells derives its origins. The earliest reference is in the Final Concords of Henry III of the 11th October 1234, where reference is made to a Peter de Ingoldmells and his wife, Alice, who may well be our earliest recorded ancestors. There is documentary evidence of the Ingamells family, individuals and their property, spanning 500 years of history. This family story begins in Tudor England.
>
> As far as can be ascertained from parish registers, the earliest traceable descendants of those Ingamells today are probably three brothers, Henry Ingamells of Saleby, Richard Ingamells of Saleby and William Ingamells of South Reston of Lincolnshire in the 1540s.

I have started this family history at the furthest point back, using the earliest evidence that I have, the wills of the three brothers. As far as it is possible to discover, my family history appears to link back to William Ingamells:

> Henry, Richard and William would have been born in the reign of the Tudor kings, maybe in the reign of King Henry VII, and would have seen the beginning and end of King Henry VIII's reign. These were both exciting and changing times in English history. Much of the world was still undiscovered and society was heavily underpinned by religion – people believed good harvests and good weather could be won by prayer, and, equally, bad harvests, storms and floods were God's retribution for some wrongdoing or lapse of faith. Indeed, Henry VIII thought that he was subject of God's retribution for marrying his brother's widow by having no surviving male heir. Events in an individual's life may have been analysed to divine (literally) God's message. Henry VIII turned his back on the Catholic Church when it denied him a divorce and he set about desecrating and demolishing the monasteries and abbeys throughout the land.
>
> This was the world that William Ingamells lived in and the events he would have lived through, and it is with him that this family history begins. We first encounter him on the 24th May 1547 making his last will and testament.

The scene is set – the historical context has been laid out and William Ingamells has been introduced to the readers using his will, the earliest documentary evidence I have.

Using Your Oral History

You can use the material obtained in any interviews you have carried out with your living relatives to develop your story further. For example, you may quote direct, saying:

> We can find out a little bit about Isaac Brown Rogers from his son Harcourt, who says of him, 'My father was about my height, about 5 foot 8. He wasn't a very big man but he was strong. He was very strict. I don't think he ever joked! He was very strict but he was also very fair. We were all scared of him.'

The interview material that you have will enable you to draw a picture for readers of what family life was like for your ancestors. You can use direct quotations such these examples by explaining who the contributor was by the use of brackets. Do not forget to name your contributors since these identifications will be particularly useful to future generations.

> [*William Rogers junior*] Our mum hit me once and it was almost as if she was hurting herself. Our dad would hit us, they used to row like blue murder because he hit us kids, she would say, 'Your hands are too big, you mustn't hit children, your hands are too heavy.' I remember she threw a cup at our dad once and it hit him on the head and she dived out of the back window! She opened the window and dived out of the back window! They used to have some terrible rows, over kids or over money but I've never known my father to raise a finger to my mother.

Choose your quotations carefully, not forgetting that what may seem ordinary to one reader will be interesting detail to another. Your main aim should be to use quotations to demonstrate how your relatives used to live.

> [*William Rogers junior*] We used to have a meal but it was nothing near substantial, you couldn't eat your fill, it would just about keep you going. So we used to go over the allotment. A Brussels sprout, you could eat that, you could also dig a spud up and bake it on a fire. We used to sit over there for hours baking spuds. I suppose in the long run we were slowly starving because we didn't have enough to eat. The peas had just started to come and so I was over there with one or two other lads and we whipped these peas off. The pods were lovely and big and full, so it was down your jumper and there was a big bulge right out there. The chap see me and we started to run and I got over my fence and I've run down but if I ran in the side door he would see me, so I've run around to the front door, knocked on the front door. Our mum said, 'What did you come round to the front door for?', and I said, 'There's a bloke chasing us'. So I've gone in the front door

and she said, 'What have you got?', I said, 'I've got a load of peas.' So she's gone to the kitchen and she's looking down the garden and the bloke's saying, 'Madam, madam, they're using your side way as a getaway.' She said, 'Yes, I know and I'm going to get the bloody Police to them in a minute!' And there's me in the kitchen with these lovely peas!

These direct quotations are excellent to use since they give a sense of actuality. Or you can use stories recounted second-hand:

[*Roy Rogers*] My father [William Cromwell Rogers] didn't used to talk a lot about his experiences of years ago, but I remember him saying that his step-mother used to treat her own children a lot better than she used to treat him and his brothers. They lived next to a viaduct. When they finished a shift in the pit they used to come home and they'd be sitting in their bedroom and they could hear a train coming through the tunnel and they used to have a bet on how many carriages was on the train by the noise it made in the tunnel. She was so mean with the food – and don't forget these were young men working down the mine – they would have a bowl of soup and a round of bread and they would cut these rounds of bread up into squares and they would have a bet on how many carriages were on a train, coming through the tunnel and whoever won obviously had a better meal than the ones that lost, and so you learned to either not have a bet or make sure you were on to a winner.

Use your photographs and postcards to illustrate your document and make it less wordy. If you use quotations from interviews, you could punctuate the text with a picture of the interviewee and photographs of a particular recalled event, if one were available, or include other characters introduced during the text. Always label your photographs so that everyone is aware of who is pictured in order to avoid any confusion.

Examine your interviewees' occupations and the conditions they may have worked under, and the tools or the methods employed at the time and introduce these to your readers, either by way of essays, as mentioned, or by writing short passages containing the information to intersperse within your story. When writing, try to imagine yourself as the reader and anticipate any questions your readers might have as they read about the lives of their ancestors and, where possible, offer explanations. If your comments are conjectural then say so in order not to mislead future generations who may take theories as fact. There is nothing wrong with speculation, but often it can end like Chinese whispers.

THE INCLUSION OF FAMILY TREES

The inclusion of your family tree is of prime importance and so it should be clearly laid out to avoid any misinterpretations. If it is extensive then use a smaller print font if it will enable the tree to fit on to one page, or print it 'landscape' instead of the more likely default 'portrait'. If you have particularly neat handwriting or are practised in calligraphy, it would add a pleasant touch to your history if you were able to write out the family tree in this way. If you wish to make it clear that there was an illegitimate birth, you should show this by creating a dotted line and adding a footnote to this effect.

Where you include the family tree in your document is a matter of personal preference, but it might be a good idea to place it at the front for ease of reference.

CHARACTERIZATIONS

How many times have you heard someone say about a person, 'Oh, he was really one of life's characters!'? Your family history is full of characters, and if you are concerned that those who read your account in years to come should have a flavour of the people you are talking about, you may wish to consider taking each family member individually and drawing up evidence as to his or her character.

For example, by using photographs, anecdotes and interview material, you could demonstrate your relative's characteristics for future readers. This will be particularly helpful if the person you are writing about is dead but still known to those alive and they are able to recount stories about the individual. Ask your relatives to describe their parents, brothers and sisters, as well the long-dead relatives they knew since this will give an interesting insight into how they saw them. It could bring them alive to new readers, rather than being just more names on the family tree.

In order to illustrate how useful this could be in providing future readers with a glimpse of the personality of an ancestor, I have gathered together in the accompanying box all the comments I have been given on my maternal great-grandmother, who died before I was born. The sources are her two daughters and two grandsons. I leave readers to draw their own conclusions as to what type of person they feel she was.

Character Sketch

Our mum was dark haired and wore glasses. Very determined woman, very fair, worked harder than a lot of men ever worked, I'll say that. She worked very, very hard, all her life. She sent us to Sunday School regularly, but she didn't believe in church herself. Mum said your church is your way of life and how you treat people. She would push the truck, a cart around the town. She would buy things and sell them. She would do that right up until about three weeks before a baby was born. When she was young, she was on the milk round and then on the trams during the war. Our mum was too independent for her own good. When our dad died, she had to go on the parish relief because he had no pension and she told them she was willing to go to work for her children, and so all they

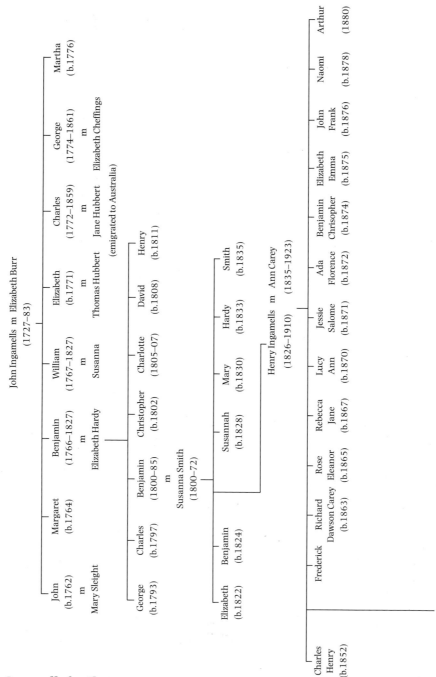

Ingamells family tree.

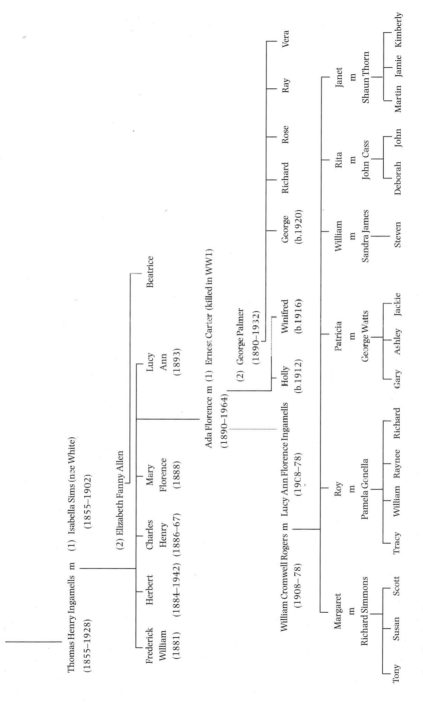

Character Sketch continued

allowed her was seven [shillings] and ninepence a week. Mum was very, very independent, very fair, very quick tempered, very quick to take umbrage, she would fall out with the neighbours in a minute. In those days, you couldn't ask your mother any questions, and if you did, you wouldn't get any answers. You daren't stand near mum if she was talking to anybody, if you went indoors and mum was talking to a neighbour and you stood there, she'd say, 'And what do you want?', 'Nothing mum', 'Then off.' She wouldn't let you listen to a conversation at all. In the winter, when we used to have coughs and colds, we had the open fire grate there, and she would send over the chemist for sixpenny worth of camphorated oil, before we went to bed we always had our chests rubbed back and front, with camphorated oil and the soles of our feet. Every Saturday we had a dose of liquorice powder to keep our bowels clear so we didn't have spots or pimples and none of us suffered with pimples or boils. It was a regular thing, this dosage of liquorice powder and it was dark, blacky green and thick! Made with warm water. We were always kept clean and well fed. At Christmas time, mum used to go round to each house to see what the children had for Christmas and always mum's house for a Christmas party. And Saturdays mum's house was always the meeting place, when the family always came in for a cup of tea. Mum's mother died when she was about 11. Her father put her in the Salvation Army Children's Home, but how long she was in there I don't know. I always remember her saying. Our mum used to work in China Town. She got lost once. She said she was terrified, there was all these Chinese, but I don't know how she found her way home. In this hotel where she worked, there was this bloke and he had this big ape, and mum said she used to be terrified to go past the door, because she could hear this ape chattering away and it would terrify her. [Daughters Holly King and Winifred Bargent]

I can remember the soldiers when they were going to D-Day, coming through the village. She was standing outside with cups of tea and biscuits and I heard her say that she hoped someone, somewhere, was doing the same for her sons, as she had Uncle Dick, Uncle George and Uncle Ray all in the Services. That was her philosophy, she was doing it for somebody's son, she hoped somebody was doing it for her sons. She seemed to adapt to village life, she got to know different people in the village. I suppose that was her way because she used to go out 'calling' on all the houses in Southsea and she could communicate with people. She was pretty fair-minded, which I think you've got to be if you've got a big family, haven't you? You've got to be fair with them all, because when they're grown up, they know whether you were fair with them or not. She used to have some smashing parties. If there was ever one of Uncle Ray's mates or Uncle George's mates they were always invited. She really enjoyed family life. She was clever really because she used to provide for them all, she used to go out 'calling' and knocking on doors and then, when she wasn't doing that, she was working for Copus. After the War, I used to go down there on Friday nights and ask her if I could sleep. I used to sleep in Uncle Ray's bed, with all nice white linen sheets. Spotless it was. Used to do a few errands for her, go and get wood for the fire, logs and that. She lived there for 25 years. I used to write to her when I was out in Aden and she used to write to me. [Grandson Roy Rogers]

> Granny Palmer, Ada, always reminded me of a strict old bird! She's nothing like my mother in temperament at all, she was just so strict that it was unreal. You wouldn't touch this and you wouldn't touch that, but I realize now, as you grow up, that you're the same, if you've got kids running around and pulling things about, you tend to say, 'Don't touch this or don't touch that.' She was either in the kitchen or in her back room sat in a wicker chair. But I had some good times up there. [Grandson William Rogers]

When you put together all the anecdotes about one person, common themes materialize and gradually his or her personality will emerge.

Sensitivity and Sentimentality

How far do you go in revealing the lives of your ancestors? If you know deep, dark secrets do you tell them? Were your ancestors all they appeared to be? Telling it how it is – or was – may be quite tricky and something you will have to consider when writing a family history.

Let us assume that your family history does not contain any such secrets – certainly none known to you, otherwise you probably would not be predisposed to write your family history in the first place. But what if you uncover something hitherto unknown and of a sensitive nature? I have managed unwittingly to shatter a few illusions that some of my family had about other members – nothing too serious, but, nevertheless, things were later not as they initially appeared to be. My mother and her sisters always remembered their paternal grandfather as a very strict disciplinarian, a deeply religious man who ran a choir and, some have said, even wrote hymns. I was not quite prepared for their reaction when I casually told them that he was illegitimate – they were disbelieving and almost appalled. 'But he was always so respectable and strict', they cried, as if this should have influenced the circumstances of his birth. Perhaps this was why he was the way he was. Following on from their reaction to this news, I trod more carefully when I received the death certificate of my maternal great-great grandmother. When I saw that it said that she had died from mania exhaustion in the imbecile ward of the local workhouse in 1902, it suddenly struck me that I might have uncovered a dark family secret. Nobody had said anything about this. What was 'mania exhaustion'? Was it hereditary? What would I tell them, how would they react to this? To my mind, it certainly could explain the perhaps more eccentric behaviour of my mother's family. Luckily, when I broke this news to my aunts they laughed and all agreed that it did indeed explain a lot! But my great-aunt, who was a whole generation nearer to this revelation, took the information more seriously and wrote in a letter to me: 'Wasn't very good information about mum's mother was it? I don't suppose mum knew about that. (Another skeleton in the cupboard let loose.)' Which illustrates how careful you will have to be when trying to gauge how people will react to the facts you may discover.

The reaction to my great grandfather's illegitimacy shows how people build up their own ideas of what a particular person was like. If your family members are anything like mine, once they do this, they quickly become sentimental over him or her, especially once they are dead. While it may be true that you should not speak ill of the dead, do you just reveal their good points and your happy memories of them, or do you reveal them warts and all? My advice would be above all to bear in mind who might be reading your history, and, if you do feel that something should be mentioned that is not altogether flattering to a particular person, try to counter it with something positive. You may find yourself playing family diplomat as you develop your story and characters. But at the same time, be aware of the sentimentality with which people will oil their stories of past events and that could ultimately make them unreliable witnesses to the past that you are asking them to recount.

FAMILY FABLES

What if you have a family legend? As when someone might say to you, 'Of course, it is said that we are descended from Mary Queen of Scots, or at least we have some connection or other with her.' Or when a relative is sure that he was told some story whereby there was money or a title in the family. How much store do you put on family legends? Is it worth commenting on them, especially if they have no verifiable basis in fact? Do you want to put them in your story?

It is perfectly legitimate to mention anything that has been passed down in the family; whether it has any basis in fact is another matter entirely. To ignore a 'story' may suggest to your readers that either you did not know about it or you have dismissed it. To take the example above, it may seem fanciful to believe in a family connection with Mary Queen of Scots, but if you mention it and explain that it is just a family legend that you either have or have not proved, it may lend credence to any research in the future that may be of a more tenable nature.

SPECIAL FEATURES

Within your family history an ancestor may have been involved in a major event, for example, the sinking of the *Titanic*, the Battle of Waterloo or the Boer War. If this was the case, you may wish to consider the creation of a special feature to set out the personal story in relation to the event.

Having discovered that my great-great grandfather drowned at sea, I detailed the circumstances of his death as a 'feature', using the information in newspaper articles and provided my readers with a full account of what must have been a tragic event for our family. In another family history I have a section dedicated to the Second World War and bring my readers' attention to the family members who served in it and to those who never returned, again providing as much detail as possible as to the circumstances of the events.

If, for example, a relative of yours died in the First World War – and such was the loss of life that relatively few families were unaffected – you might wish to give this relative a special place in your story. As an example of what you could include, Lt Lionel Clegg, aged 21, married his fiancée Doris Fowler in June 1918 before returning to France. An officer of the 7th Battalion of the Tank Corps, he was killed in action on 22 August, less than three months before the end of the war. He is buried in Gommecourt Cemetery No. 2, opened in 1917 when the battlefields were cleared. If you have a relative who died in similar circumstances, research at the National Archives could provide you with such details as a copy of the telegram informing the next of kin of the death, letters containing details of war pensions, and perhaps, as in the illustration, a list of the personal effects returned.

The message reads: 'Deeply regret Lieut L Clegg 7th Bttln Tanks Killed in Action August Twenty Second – Army Command express regret.'

These documents are particularly poignant since the telegram was received by Clegg's mother and the list of personal effects includes photographs – perhaps of his new wife and other family members – and private letters. Documents such as these give presence to a life cut short and will provide you with an opportunity for further research in order to bring distant relatives to life for future readers.

You may also wish to consider a special feature section if a relative had a particularly long and distinguished career – perhaps they were musical or artistic – where his or her achievements could be mapped out.

Personal effects in possession of Lt Lionel Clegg and returned on his death.

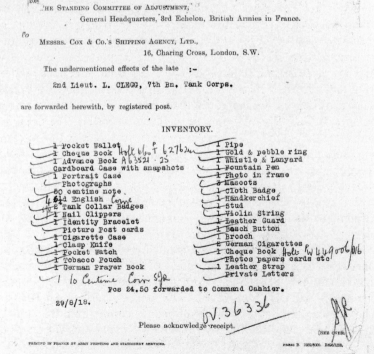

WHERE DOES THE STORY END?

If you begin your story at its most distant point in time and end with the here and now, this will mean that you can, should you wish, update your history easily as to future births, deaths and marriages. Therefore your story will remain 'open-ended.' Equally, by virtue of the fact that there is probably either little or no documented evidence of the identity of your earliest ancestors, the 'beginning' is also open-ended. Your story, however, will need some form of an end. You therefore may wish to consider completing your story with either a conclusion or a summary chapter.

In a concluding chapter you can take an overview of your family story, draw some conclusions about it and summarize your family's history. For instance, consider the fact that even if your research into the past has its evidential limits which only allow you to go back 100, 150 or 200 years, your family's history, in fact, spans back into the depths of time or else you would not be here today. Unless your ancestors were very popular or very important the chances are that they will not have left any documentary traces behind. The legacy was, of course, the siring of the next generation. You may wish to remind your readers of this (especially if your family history is limited) and, as added interest, speculate on who they were and where they may have come from – the Normans, the Anglo-Saxons, the Vikings or even the Romans.

The origins of your family name may help you to take your readers further back than they may otherwise have expected. If, for example, you can relate your surname geographically, you could hitch your genealogical wagon to a Viking invader or a Saxon warrior. While you might think it fanciful to speculate on your origins 1,000 or 2,000 years ago, now it is becoming an increasingly topical subject and people are interested to know of what race they are and the geographical location that their ancestors may have come from and are thus willingly supplying their DNA to help to find those results. Since the Y chromosome is found only in male lines, it is also now possible to link people now alive with their most distant ancestors. I do not advocate that you should set out to mislead your readers, especially your future readers, by speculating on these ancestors, but as long as you state that it is only speculation, there is no harm in firing their imaginations in the conclusion of your story. The fact remains that you did have an ancestor who lived at the time of William the Conqueror and one who either was one or witnessed the Vikings invading in 800; 2,000 years ago your ancestors were as much alive as you are today.

You could draw on history books to observe life and times throughout the Dark Ages to speculate on who your ancestors were at the time of the last millennium. It is interesting to note that in medieval times the forenames most commonly used were John, William, Thomas, Richard, Roger, Henry and Peter. The chances are that at least one of your ancestors from this time had one of these names, and thus, if you wanted to, you could stick your neck out for the end of your story and have some fun and name a probable early ancestor.

Domesday Book was the result of a survey completed across England in 1086–87, and, as well as detailing possessions and lands, gave a head count of those then living and working. Your ancestors were likely to have been among them. For example, the Vikings (comprising Danes, Norwegians and Swedes) raided the coasts of England, Scotland, Ireland, France, Spain and even Italy from 800. Before the Vikings, the Saxons (ancient Germanic tribes) overran the Roman shore forts from 400 and set about destroying Roman Britain. The Romans had occupied Britain since 43 and had recruits in their armies from across their vast empire, bringing multicultured peoples to the shores of a land previously occupied solely by indigenous tribesmen. Your ancestors came from one of these cultures and managed to survive generation after generation for you to be here today. To quote again from Debrett's *Guide to Tracing Your Ancestry*, in his introduction, Sir Iain Moncreiffe makes the point:

> ...never forget that you each owe your very existence not just to your parents, but to *every single one* of your personal ancestors since mankind began. It is impossible to knock out one brief link at any time in history and keep the whole chain together ... if William the Conqueror had never been born as William the Bastard, illegitimate son of the original Harlot (Harlotte of Falaise), the tanner's attractive daughter to whose prowess in bed one single night in 1027 so many of us thus owe our very being. All our ancestors' lives are interesting, for they were all necessary in handing down life to us even if they lived long, long ago.

Speculate on where your ancestors, may have come from – did they come over with the French with William in 1066, were they servants or soldiers of exotic Roman ancestry, or fearsome, hairy, Nordic invaders? You probably will not be too wide of the mark if you stick to just these categories; in fact, as your ancestors married and mated throughout the coming centuries, all these possibilities and more will probably have become part of your genetic make-up. Just as the Vikings and the Saxons colonized England, the Spanish, French, Portuguese and English colonized parts of America, Africa and Australia ensuring that the genetics of the peoples in these countries really are multiracial.

As an illustration of how you might conclude your story in this way, the passage in the accompanying box is from the last pages of one of my own family histories.

CREATING SUPPLEMENTS AND APPENDICES

You have the main body of your story, telling the journey your ancestors made through the centuries, but how will you easily get access to those tricky dates of birth, death and marriage for each of them and keep up with their names and places of birth?

You could add an appendix or supplement to the main story in which you could include your family tree, if you have not included one already, copies of

Conclusion

This short history is a snapshot of this family spanning almost 200 years and, despite the opening chapter being entitled 'The Beginning', there is, in fact, no real beginning, just as there is also no end to this story. And whilst it may be disappointing to some in its length of only 200 years, it should be remembered that the Casses here today contain many of the characteristics of those who lived and bore their name 200, 300 or 400 years ago. The only difference is that in the last 200 years people's lives have been more diligently recorded than in previous centuries. Unfortunately, the omission of just one inky name scratched by the nib of a quill pen in a parish register can break the link and ability for us to trace the chain with our ancestors.

Despite the lack of documentary evidence, it is a fact that our ancestors lived during the Great Fire of London and the reign of the first Queen Elizabeth, as well as the times of William the Conqueror and the Saxon and the Roman invasion – the proof of this is from those alive today.

There is a lot of speculation about the Cass name. It could easily have started out as 'Case' and just as easily have been from the French 'Casse' (as those on the Isle of Wight believe), or from the Irish 'O'Casey', or more exotically from the Trojan prophetess Cassandra, as many of the surname books state. Were they originally from Ireland, or did they come over with the Romans, or were they from Spain or France originally? Our ancestors could have come from all these countries.

As the twenty-first century begins, it is perhaps an interesting realization that you can put this family history alongside social history and know something about ancestors who lived through those times. In the first millennium, up to the year 1000, a Cass ancestor was roaming around somewhere, either here in England, in Ireland or in France, surviving the slings and arrows of the time. We may not know their names nor what they looked like, but their trials and tribulations and changing fortunes would not have differed far from those of the Casses documented here in the past 200 years. And the fact that we are here to day means that our ancestors lived and survived through all the events of the last 1,000 years and before, bringing us here to where we are today.

transcripts of interviews, full and unabridged versions, transcriptions of original documents and copies of wills and other certificates. This will also help to preserve your original documents. You could also consider using the supplement or appendix to add notes about your research and theories, rather than try to explain your methods of research or your inability to find anything more about an ancestor in your story. In this way, the story itself remains 'pure' and not clogged with this material. It may also aid future readers if they are were to follow your lines of research and your explanations of any dead ends you met.

It is worth keeping your story and sources separate as the story may get lost in among transcriptions of original documents. You could also use a summary to explain why you were not able to pursue your research as far back you would have liked, whether this be due to, for instance, lack of available records, an illegitimate birth or migration to another part of the country. You could also use this section to explain surname origins and make clear to your readers any information that is purely speculative or only hearsay.

6 PRODUCING YOUR STORY

BEGINNING

Once you have your material, how do you present it to your readers?

The style of writing you use is up to you; it may be more a case of catering for many family members, and whether you inject it with humour and speculation for fun or keep it strictly factual, or a mixture of both is a choice you can make when considering your audience. You may wish to present the material as an autobiography, with you telling the story in the first person and inserting your comments and opinions alongside those of your interviewees. Should you choose this method, use your memories well and include small details, not neglecting things such as evocative smells and sounds. If this seems too ambitious for you, simply tell your story as you yourself would like to read it, as if you had had it written for you.

You should also consider the format your work will have: will it be handwritten it or will you use a computer or typewriter? Writing your story by hand will personalize it for the reader but handwriting has the disadvantage of having to be passed round from reader to reader, unless you studiously make several copies. You should also consider the legibility of your hand. And then there is the risk that your manuscript may get lost.

I recommend the use of a computer since it will make it possible for you to format the document in any way you like, change or add to it at any time, and 'import' pictures, family trees and borders easily, and make the best use of many different fonts and styles. You will also be able to email copies to interested relatives – for instance, circulating draft sections for others to comment on, add to or amend with the addition of new material or photographs – while always keeping the original safe with you. (It is also worth remembering that computers may be hired as you might hire a television, so an expensive outlay can be avoided.)

If this is your preferred option, you may consider creating the story of your family by the use of Microsoft Powerpoint™ (incorporated in the Microsoft Office™ package) or some similar software. With a scanner you could combine text, graphics and sound to present the story as a slide show. By creating a Powerpoint production of your story, you could produce a very polished product and a hard copy can still be printed off.

You can use your computer to store and enhance your photographs. Computer programs now make it easy for the novice to tidy up cracked and marked photographs. Some time spent learning your way around your preferred word processing software will enable you to use photographs to illustrate your document, enabling you to embed them in text by utilizing the 'wrap round' facility whereby text can sit beside photographs to give a more professional finish to your history.

There are also many software packages that offer ways of assembling and displaying a family tree which could be an embellishment of your story.

But however you decide to use your computer, I would stress the importance of making a regular back-up copy of your work in the event of a power surge or inadvertent file deletion. It may even be useful to keep your backed-up files away from your machine and possibly even with a relative or friend. Equally important is the installation of up-to-date anti-virus software to avoid an 'attack' on your machine the risk of a loss of your work.

SPELLING AND GRAMMAR

It is important to stress that, when writing your story, you should not let any fears you may have about your spelling or grammar put you off from completing your project, or even beginning it, for that matter.

Naturally you will want to produce a work of which you can feel proud and the use of a computer therefore may be a saviour if you lack confidence in this area. Your word processing program will incorporate a spellchecker and can also be set to highlight obvious grammatical errors. (But remember to set the program's default 'language' at the correct version of English.) You should also arm yourself with a good dictionary, a thesaurus and, if you really fear offending your readers, a guide to English grammar.

Just as importantly, if your education has been of the best, try to resist the temptation to display this fact through the use of words that will have your readers reaching for their dictionaries. You should aim to use sentences that simply say what you mean, in other words use plain English. Look in your newspaper to see how the sentences are written and how the message is conveyed. Keep your sentences from being overlong and complex in structure so that readers do not have to restart the sentence when they get to the end of it to understand what you are trying to say.

It is also a good idea to let others read a draft of your story, as suggested earlier, to check for any spelling errors and obvious grammatical faux pas, but the message is: do not get too hung up on your split infinitives and negative auxiliaries.

Getting the family history down in writing should take primacy over correct spelling and grammar. How many of us would give our eye-teeth to be given facts about our family that we previously knew nothing about – would we really choose to criticize the spelling of notes written in a family Bible or other documented family history?

CREATIVE WRITING

You may feel that, despite the sentiments above, your skills currently make writing your family history beyond your capability. There are, first, books available for the budding writer which will steer you through the intricacies of sentence and paragraph construction and, should you go public, the publishing arena (*see* p.109). Next, if you do feel a lack of confidence and that a book is an insufficient help, you may wish to consider a creative writing course to help you. Such courses tend to be short, available locally and encouraging to the novice writer. Begin writing your story and, if you feel that you need more assistance, enrol on a course where you can obtain advice on your work and encouragement. Above all, remember that it is the content that your readers are really interested in, and it is this fact that you should keep in mind.

There are also alternative approaches. First, if you can identify a relative who could help you, you may consider a collaborative production. Or a writing group may help you in you endeavour to produce a family history and a list of these can be found at www.writer-circles.com

WORD SIZE AND FONT

If you use a computer, be mindful of the word size and the font you employ in your document when considering your readers, some of whom may be elderly; thus you may wish to consider one-and-a-half or double line spacing. Try to avoid fancy fonts, Old English style is in keeping with the project and will give your document a period feel, but unless you use a large sized font it will be difficult to read. If you really like this style, you could begin your story using Old English for the titles with the first letter or word of the text in large, bold print, as shown in the box below.

The Beginning – Shaftesbury – Dorset

In 1814 *Charles Cass was born in Shaftesbury, a small but important historical market town in the beautiful rolling hills of the Blackmore Vale in Dorset. He was baptized at the old Holy Trinity Church on the 21st August 1814, the illegitimate son of Ann Cass, a labourer.*

If you use a computer you may also take advantage of a desktop publishing software package, although this is by no means an essential element in creating an interesting and readable document.

You may decide to keep to what is probably your word processor's default page format of A4 landscape (either double-sided or single-sheet), which will enable you to get a lot of information on a page, including photographic material.

CHAPTERS OR PARTS?

In order to separate the different periods of your relatives' lives you may consider splitting the story into parts or chapters. For example, the start could simply be called The Beginning, then Early Life, Life in the 1920s and War Years, any heading that describes a particular time in their lives that you have information on. This will help to develop and define your story as it takes shape and you gather more information, as in this passage:

The First World War

Harry Cass was 28 years old when the First World War broke out in 1914.

On the 1st February 1917 until the 23rd May 1917, he is shown as working as a stoker on HMS *Victory II*. On the 24th May 1917, until the 6th March 1919 (when he was demobilized) he worked on board HMS *King George V*, a super dreadnought battleship of 23,000 tons, 555 feet long and carrying ten 13^1/$_2$-inch guns, twenty-four 4-inch guns and three 21-inch torpedo tubes.

His war record shows his date and place of birth and tell us that he was 5 foot 10 inches tall.

My own history uses the following named parts, for example:

The Beginning: Dorset	The Beginning: Lincolnshire
The Early Years	Tudor Beginnings
Migration to Portsmouth	Stuart Monarchs and Cromwell's Republic
First World War	The Impact of the Enclosure Act
Family Life	The Fenlands
Second World War	Migration to Portsmouth
Family Life	First World War
Summary	Family Life
	Second World War
	Return to Family Life
	Summary

Equally, you could set out each significant change in period in chapters, preceded by a contents list, as in:

Chapter 1 The Birth of Charles Cass
Chapter 2 The Marriage of Charles Cass and Caroline Tanswell
Chapter 3 Family Life
Chapter 4 Charles and Caroline Cass – End of an Era
Chapter 4 Migration to Portsmouth
Chapter 5 Death at Sea

The good thing is, it is entirely your choice – with consideration for your readers, of course.

DESIGNING YOUR COVER

Design the cover of your book by using your computer – you are limited only by your own imagination. You may wish to keep it simple and just have the name of your family on the front in bold lettering – *The Cass Family History*. Alternatively, you can include graphics (there is probably a wealth of clipart to pick from included with your word processor for use) or family photographs. A pleasant touch might be to use the image of a tree and display it as a watermark, which would enable you to write your title across it. And do not forget the author's name on the front too.

BINDING

How you bind your document is also a matter of personal choice. If your document is in draft form, you may wish to use thick card as a cover while you pass the document around among your relatives before you make your final copy. You might like, as an alternative, to bind your final document by using a protective, plastic cover, or have it ring-bound or heat-sealed. All these options are fairly readily available through stationers and other outlets.

If you wish your document to have a more permanent 'book' binding you will need to consider whether to have a soft paperback style or a hardback format. The latter would be the more durable, but the former would be slightly cheaper and perhaps more portable. Finally, you may wish to consider a book-binding course that would eventually give your book a truly original, personal touch.

PUBLISHING YOUR STORY

Whether you have decided to write your family history just for yourself or for distribution solely among other family members, if you have access to the internet do not neglect the possibility of publishing your history on your own website. But if, after all your efforts, you feel that your story deserves a more permanent place on your bookshelf, there are some options open to you.

Small Print Runs
Small book-printing presses will do short runs – at a cost, of course – but if you feel that this is how you would like to present your book, you could determine your family's interest by asking whether they would subscribe to it, thereby help with the cost and sponsor their own copies. There are publishers advertising this service in family history magazines, or you may consider contacting local publishers.

But before you leap into this option, consider whether you have as much information for your story as you could reasonably expect. To uncover new facts which would add to the story after you have chosen this route might prove expensive to update copies and will make you wish that you had waited just a little longer. As regards this possibility, it may be worth including a few blank sheets at the end of the volume so that family members can update the book with details of futher events or more anecdotes. If this method of publication does become an option, you may also wish to list your sponsors at the front or the back of the book, which would personalize it more for the recipients.

Self-Publishing

If you think that your story has general interest and you would like to reach a wider audience than your immediate family, you may wish to consider self-publishing. This will not only provide you with a professionally-produced book but you will also have an ISBN number issued for it, thus enabling your work to be ordered in bookshops and it will also be subject to copyright.

There are a number of publishers offering this service and their advertisements can be found in newspapers, in writing and family history magazines and on the internet. For the purposes of publishing a family history, the best route may be a print-on-demand service. The publishers of these can offer a full editing and publishing service for a fixed fee. Books may be made available both on-line and in hard copy according to the demand, hence the title 'print on demand'. In this way you do not have to pay for expensive print runs and have 500 plus books to find space for in your spare room, let alone sell them to recoup your outlay. Traditional publishers will run off an agreed print run, and, usually, the more they print, the lower the cost. Before you go down this route, ask the publisher to show you what a crate of 3,000 copies of your book might look like; when the lorry turns up at your house with them you will have to find the space to store them and they may hang around for some time. Shorter print runs may be more expensive, but, in the end, far easier to deal with.

Should you go down this route, ensure that you work out your costings, and, unless you plan to market your book vigorously, you should be prepared to make a loss on the venture; in that way any profit or the recovery of costs will be a bonus.

Publishers will usually give you tips on your marketing strategy, which will include local press releases to explain and advertise your book, how to make contact with local, independent booksellers and ideas about the location and timing of a full-blown book launch.

If this is your preferred option, take care in choosing your publisher and always seek to find references from their previous authors.

Mainstream Publishers

It is unlikely in today's market that a mainstream publisher would be interested in publishing your family history. Having said this, *Angela's Ashes*, the childhood memoirs of Frank McCourt, based in Limerick in the 1930s, has sold 5 million copies around the world and been produced as a film. On a smaller but no less entertaining scale, *The Road to Nab End* by William Woodruff, describing his childhood in Blackburn from 1916, was published by Abacus, an imprint of Times Warner Books UK. Publishing is not an exact science, just as family history is not all about dates and documents. If you produce a story with enough human interest to attract a mainstream publisher then you can congratulate yourself and, as these two examples illustrate, that is possible. As has been said before here, it is the small details of people's everyday lives that readers can empathize with that will humanize your story and make it real for your readers.

THE END PRODUCT: THE HISTORY OF YOUR FAMILY

Your family history is literally a 'living' document, ready to be updated and added to as and when information becomes available. Even with scant material you can still write a reasonable account of each relative's life and times. Those with more fully documented lives should provide you with enough material to write a fairly comprehensive history, punctuating the bare facts of times and dates with photographs, picture postcards, essays, anecdotes, diaries and letters to give your ancestors their full presence in your history.

If you write your story including in it yourself and your children, then your story is always going to be without any real ending, in which case you will be the last relative to be written about, or you may choose to finish it with your parents. Wherever you choose to end, once you have finished it – if a family history can ever be finished – you may rest assured that the rest of the family will clamour to read it.

FURTHER READING

Listed below are books which are useful in understanding the past and how your ancestors may have lived.

General History Reference Books

Domesday Book – A Complete Translation (Penguin) (ISBN 0 140 51535 6)

Harry Batsford and Charles Fry, *The English Cottage* (Batsford)

Richard Britnell, *Daily Life in the Late Middle Ages* (Sutton Publishing) (ISBN 0 7509 1587 1)

Thomas Burke, *Travel in England* (Batsford)

Michael Flynn, *The Second Fleet: Britain's Grim Convict Armada of 1790* (ISBN 0 908120 83 4)

J.L. and Barbara Hammond, *The Village Labourer* (Longman)

Christopher Hibbert, *The English: A Social History 1066–1945* (Guild Publishing)

Pamela Horn, *The Rise and Fall of the Victorian Servant* (Sutton Publishing)

W.G. Hoskins, *Local History in England* (Longman) (ISBN 0 582 49371 4)

Gertrude Jekyll and Sydney R. Jones, *Old English Household Life* (Batsford)

Robert Lacey and Danny Danziger, *The Year 1000* (Little, Brown)

Lloyd and Jennifer Laing, *Medieval Britain* (Herbert Press) (ISBN 1 871569 84 2)

Peter Laslett, *The World We Have Lost – Further Explored* (ISBN 0 416 35350 9)

Anne Laurence, *Women in England 1500–1760: A Social History* (Phoenix) (ISBN 1 84212 622 9)

Henrietta Leyser, *Medieval Women: A Social History of Women in England 450–1500* (Phoenix) (ISBN 1 84212 621 0)

Peter Moss, *Town Life Through the Ages* (Harrap) (ISBN 0 245 59824 3)

Lionel Munby, *How Much Is That Worth?* (Phillimore) (ISBN 0 8503 3741 0)

Camille Naish, *Death Comes to the Maiden: Sex and Execution 1431–1933* (Routledge) (ISBN 0 415 05585 7)

Liza Picard, *Dr Johnson's London* (Phoenix) (ISBN 1 84212 437 4)

Liza Picard, *Restoration London* (Phoenix) (ISBN 1 84212 467 6)

Ivy Pinchbeck, *Women Workers and the Industrial Revolution 1750–1850* (Virago)

Peter Quennell, *London's Underworld (Selections from London Labour and the London Poor)* (Spring Books)

Peter Quennell, *Mayhew's Characters* (William Kimber)

Jasper Ridley, *The Tudor Age* (Guild Publishing)

Simon Schama, *A History of Britain: At the Edge of the World? 3000BC – AD1603* (BBC Worldwide) (ISBN 0 563 38497 2)

Paul Slack, *The Impact of the Plague in Tudor and Stuart England* (Routledge & Kegan Paul) (ISBN 0 7102 0469 8)

Francis W. Stear, *Farm and Cottage Inventories of Mid Essex 1635–1749* Phillimore

Roger Virgoe, *Illustrated Letters of the Paston Family* (Macmillan) (ISBN 0 333 48099 6)

Genealogy Reference Books
David Annal, *Getting Started in Family History* (National Archives) (ISBN 1 8731 6287 1)

Nick Barratt, *Tracing the History of Your House* (National Archives) (ISBN 1 9033 6522 8)

Jean Cole and John Titford, *Tracing Your Family Tree* (Countryside Books) (ISBN 1 85306 448 3)

Noel Currer-Briggs and Royston Gambier, *Debrett's Guide to Tracing Your Ancestry* (Macmillan) (ISBN 0 3333 4036 1)

D.M. Field, *Tracing Your Ancestors* (Treasure Press) (ISBN 1 8505 1195 0)

Terrick V.H. FitzHugh, *The Dictionary of Genealogy* (A. & C. Black) (ISBN 0 7136 4859 7)

Simon Fowler and William Spencer, *Army Records for Family Historians* (Countryside Books) (ISBN 1 873 16204 9)

Simon Fowler, *Tracing Your First World War Ancestors* (Countryside Books) (ISBN 1 85306 791 1)

J. Gibson and C. Rogers, *Coroners' Records in England and Wales*

John Greenham, *Tracing Your Irish Ancestors* (National Archives) (ISBN 0 7172 796 6)

Mark D. Herber, Ancestral Trails: *The Complete Guide to British Genealogy and Family History* (Sutton Publishing Society of Genealogists) (ISBN 0 7509 2484 5)

David Hey, *Family Names and Family History* (Hambledon and London) (ISBN 1 85285 255 0)

David Hey, *The Oxford Companion to Local and Family History* (Oxford University Press)

David Hey, *The Oxford Guide to Family History* (Oxford University Press) (ISBN 0 19 280313 1)

Cecil R. Humphery-Smith, *Atlas and Index of Parish Registers* (Phillimore) (ISBN 1 8607 7239 0)

Caroline Peacock, *thegoodwebguide Genealogy* (Good Web Guide) (ISBN 1 903283 06 3)

John Richardson, *The Local Historian's Encyclopedia* (Historical Publications) (ISBN 0 948667 83 4)

Don Steel, *Discovering Your Family History* (BBC) (ISBN 0 5632 1222 5)

John Titford, *Searching for Surnames* (Countryside Books) (ISBN 1 8530 6765 2)

Useful Aids to Writing
Julia Bell and Paul Magrs, *The Creative Writing Coursebook* (Macmillan) (ISBN 0 3337 8225 9)

Carole Blake, *From Pitch to Publication* (Macmillan) (ISBN 0 3337 1435 0)

Michael Legat, *Writing for a Living* (A. & C. Black) (ISBN 0 7136 5398 1)

Periodicals
Family History Monthly (Diamond Publishing)

Family Tree Magazine (ABM Publishing)

Practical Family History (ABM Publishing), **www.family-tree.co.uk**

Writing Magazine (Writers' News), **www.writingmagazine.co.uk**

Your Family Tree (Future Publishing), **www.futurenet.com/futureonline/tree**

FURTHER INFORMATION

British and Irish Resources

British Library, 96 Euston Road, London NW1 2DB **www.bl.uk**

British Library Newspaper Library, Colindale Avenue, London, NW9 5HE **www.bl.uk/collections/newspapers.html**

Church of the Latter-day Saints Family History Centre, 64–68 Exhibition Road, South Kensington, London, SW7 2PA **www.ldsorg.uk/genealogy/fhc**

The Family Records Centre 1 Myddleton Street, London, EC1R 1UW **www.familyrecords.gov.uk/frc**

Federation of Family History Societies, PO Box 2425, Coventry, CV5 6YX **www.ffhs.org.uk** email: info@ffhs.org.uk

General Register Office (Ireland), Joyce House, 8–11 Lombard Street East, Dublin 2 **www.groireland.ie**

General Register Office Scotland, New Register House, 3 West Register Street, Edinburgh EH1 3YT **www.gro-scotland.gov.uk** and **www.scotlandspeople.gov.uk**

The Guild of One Name Studies (GOONS), Box G, 14 Charterhouse Buildings, Goswell Road, London, EC1M 7BA **www.one-name.org**

Huguenot Society, Huguenot Library, University College, Gower Street, London WC1E 6BT **www.ucl.ac.uk/library/huguenot.htm**

Jewish Genealogical Society of Great Britain, PO Box 13288, London N3 3WD **www.jgsgb.org.uk/index.shtml**

Principle Probate Registry for the Family Division, First Avenue House, 42–49 High Holborn, London WC1V 6NP

National Archives (formerly Public Record Office) Ruskin Avenue, Kew, Richmond, Surrey TW9 4DU **www.nationalarchives.gov.uk**

National Archives of Ireland, Bishop Street, Dublin 8
  www.nationalarchives.ie

National Archives of Scotland, HM General Register House, 2 Princes Street,
  Edinburgh EH1 3YY **www.nas.gov.uk**

Public Record Office of Northern Ireland, 66 Balmoral Avenue, Belfast
  BT9 6NY **proni.nics.gov.uk**

Society of Genealogists, 14 Charterhouse Buildings, Goswell Road, London
  EC1M 7BA **www.sog.org.uk**

Ordnance Survey, Romsey Road, Southampton SO16 4GU
  www.ordnancesurvey.co.uk

National Library of Wales, Aberystwyth, SY23 3BU **www.llgc.org.uk**

Sources for Military History

National Archives, Ruskin Avenue, Kew, Richmond, Surrey TW9 4D
  www.nationalarchives.gov.uk

Commonwealth War Graves Commission, 2 Marlow Road, Maidenhead,
  Berkshire SL6 7DX **www.cwgc.org**

National Maritime Museum, Romney Road, Greenwich, London SE10 9NF
  www.nmm.ac.uk

Royal Naval Museum, Buildings 1–7,College Road, HM Naval Base,
  Portsmouth PO1 3LJ **www.royalnavalmuseum.org**

Army Medals Office, East Office Buildings, Droitwich, Worcs WR9 8AU

Royal Marines Historical Records and Medals, Centurion Building, Grange
  Road, Gosport, Hants PO14 9XA **www.mod.uk**

Imperial War Museum, Department of Documents, Lambeth Road, London
  SE1 6HZ **www.iwm.org.uk/Lambeth/famhist.htm**

RAF Museum, Grahame Park Way, Hendon, London NW9 5LL
  www.rafmuseum.org.uk

Australian War Memorial **www.awm.gov.au**

National Archives and Library of Canada
  www.archives.ca/02/020106_e.html

Websites for Researching Overseas Family Histories

Australia
www.cohsoft.com.au/afhc

www.naa.gov.au

www.alphalink.com.au/~aigs

www.cyndislist.com

www.australiagenweb.org/

Canada
www.archives.ca

www.cadvision.com/traces

www.cyndislist.com

Europe
www.eegsociety.org

www.cyndislist.com

www.feefhs.org

Jamaica
www.jamaicanfamilysearch.com

New Zealand
www.rootsweb.com/~nzlwgw

www.cyndislist.com

North America
www.genhomepage.com

www.familysearch.org

www.cyndislist.com

www.rootsweb.com

www.ancestry.com

www.genealogy.com

India
http://genforum/genealogy.com/india

http://nationalarchives.nic.in

International
www.genealogylinks.net

Other Useful Websites for Family Historians
1901 Census online **www.census.pro.gov.uk**
The 1901 census available on line to search, although a small fee is payable to access results.

Genes Connected **www.genesconnected.co.uk**
This site takes its lead from the successful Friends Reunited site. In the same way, it is possible to submit details of your family tree to see whether you are contacted by someone with the same family interests.

Free Birth Death and Marriage Certificates **www.freebdm.rootsweb.com**
This site has partial listings of birth, marriage and death certificates that you can freely access if you are lucky enough to find your ancestors among the records held.

www.1837online.com
Unlike the website above, this site is not free but does have a full listing and for £5 you may have fifty viewings of the records.

London Gazette **www.gazettes.online.co.uk**
This free website contains the names of those who were made bankrupt, appoint-ments in the Church and the armed forces, as well as medals won, awards and grants of peerage, naturalization and changes of name.

Writers' Circles **www.writers-circles.com**
This website contains contact address for writers' groups in your area.

Mass Observation Archive **www.sussex.ac.uk/library/massobs**
Check with your relatives to ask whether they wrote for the archive and obtain per-mission to read their responses.

Francis Frith Photographs **www.francisfrith.co.uk**
Source for old photographs.

John Howard **http://richest.org.htwm/jails/jails.html**
Details of prison life in the eighteenth century may be found here.

1881 **census www.familyrecords.gov.uk**.
Free searches can be made of the 1881 census at this, the Family Records Centre website.

www.genuki.org.uk
This site has an enormous collection of family history data with its own newsletter covering the UK and Ireland.

www.genesearch.com
A useful website with lots of links to other genealogical sites.

www.ancestry.com
This site boasts 'the largest collection of family history records on the web'.

Dorset Online Parish Clerks **www.dorset-opc.com**
The Online Parish Clerks (OPCs) are volunteers who transcribe all available histori-cal data they can find on a parish and make it freely available to researchers. There are links to the Cornwall and Devon OPC lists, which include transcriptions of parish

registers and a monumental inscriptions database. An extremely useful suite for anyone with UK Westcountry ancestry.

Mapped Out **www.allmappedout**.com or telephone 01600 869009.
Mapped Out are specialists in old Ordnance Survey maps and sell both originals and reproductions of old, large-scale maps dating form 1817–1938. They have an archive of over 20,000 maps showing place names, old toll roads, drovers tracks and, on larger maps, field boundaries, acreage, old wells, springs and barns.

INDEX